WHY CAN'T ANYONE HEAR ME?

GUIDE TO ADOLESCENT ENRICHMENT
Teen Issues/Self-Esteem Program
(companion tool to *Why Can't Anyone Hear Me?)*

TEEN ISSUES STUDENT WORKBOOK
Consumable Workbook for Self-Esteem Program

SIGMUND SAYS
A Lighter Look at Freud Through His Id, Ego, and Super-Ego

WHY DO KIDS NEED FEELINGS?
A Guide to Healthy Emotions

WORKING TOGETHER
Video Tape on Participative Management

STRESS REDUCTION TRAINING
Deep Relaxation Audio Tape

WHY CAN'T ANYONE HEAR ME?

A Guide for Surviving Adolescence

∽

Written and Illustrated by

MONTE ELCHONESS, Ph.D.

MONROE PRESS
VENTURA, CALIFORNIA

Library of Congress Cataloging in Publication Data

Elchoness, Monte
    Why can't anyone hear me?
    Bibliography: p.
    Includes index.
    1. Adolescence.   2. Adolescent psychology
    3. Parent and Child.   I. Title
HQ796.E523   1986   305.2'35   86-737
ISBN 0-936781-06-8

Printed in the United States of America
Second Edition

Cover Design by Tim Rinker

To the memory of
my mother Dora,
my father David
and
my brother Irving

ACKNOWLEDGMENTS

In completing this work which has been so meaningful to me, I wish to recognize and to offer my sincere thanks to those who helped me.

To my loving wife Dorothy who has stood by my side, providing me with inspiration, supportive encouragement, objective feedback, and much editing assistance, I say, "Take joy in this book as I do, for without you this book might not exist."

To my adult friends Susan Merrill, Jeanne Poling, and Roz Walker, I thank them for responding so generously to my request for a fresh look. Their comments and editing help was most valuable. They have reinforced my belief that when a task needs to be performed, busy people are the ones most willing to respond.

To my teen-age friends Brad Packer (who also happens to be my stepson), Chris York, and Jordan Moore, I thank them for reading my manuscript in its early stage, correcting my spelling on occasion, and providing me with the valuable views of the teenager.

I also want to thank my daughter Nancy for her generous assistance in the indexing of this book.

CONTENTS

PREFACE

This revised edition of *Why Can't Anyone Hear Me?* includes relevant information on current issues reflecting the continuing changes in society as they relate to young people and their families. A section has been included on divorce and family communication as it relates to divorce and step-parenting. This subject is a major factor affecting many children and their parents today.

My belief has been affirmed regarding the use of storytelling in *Why Can't Anyone Hear Me?* The positive feedback received indicates how the story effectively stimulates reader interest while communicating the issues. I am pleased by the wide acceptance of *Why Can't Anyone Hear Me?* and the *Guide to Adolescent Enrichment* (teacher/counselor curriculum) which are being used nationwide as a

Teen Issues/Self-Esteem program.

My purpose in writing *Why Can't Anyone Hear Me?* was prompted by my own experience of raising two daughters (now in their thirties) and surviving their adolescence. I find myself reliving this exciting and sometimes difficult process, as I now share this experience with my sixteen-year-old stepson. One might say that living through these times might be reason enough to write about it. However, not all parents who have been exposed to the teen years choose to write a book on this period.

Why then have I chosen to spend a few years of my life writing about adolescence? As a psychotherapist and a father, I felt there was more that needed to be said regarding the parent/teen relationship. I also felt the message should be directed at both young people and their parents, rather than one group or the other.

In my work I have counseled many young people referred to me by their parents and by law enforcement agencies. These young people had either broken the law, were runaways or had some form of behavior problems. In those cases where parents sent their children to me, often their plea was the same: "Please do something about my child's uncontrollable behavior." Many of my teenage clients felt the same way; they also would have liked to have sent their parents to me for some form of magical change.

Problems affecting young adults are often family related. If young people are to be helped, the complete interaction within their family must be considered. This does not mean that anyone is to blame, either parent or child. Instead, the problem itself, if there is one, should be thought of as a family concern.

Feeling strongly about the cry of frustration from many young people and their parents has encouraged me to write *Why Can't Anyone Hear Me?* Also being a witness to the negativity which seems to dominate the adolescent period, I saw the need for presenting a more positive view. It is important for the reader to understand that adolescence is a natural time of growth and change, and that there are things which can be done to make this experience easier for all who are involved. Some tools have been provided to help parents and teens communicate with one another. These tools, when used without blame and/or guilt, can help improve communication and strengthen the parent/teen relationship.

I recognize that developing an understanding between the two age groups and reducing their frustration is a tall order for any book. However, any goal must be approached one step at a time. Communication concerns are no different; they too can only be helped by understanding the problem and being willing to make changes.

This book was written for teens and parents to read, relate to, and then talk about. My hope is that you will enjoy *Why Can't Anyone Hear Me?* and find it helpful in making your family's adolescent period an adventure instead of a disaster.

Monte Elchoness

INTRODUCTION

This book is for and about young adults and the significant others in their lives: their parents, their friends and their teachers, with whom they relate on a daily basis. The period of adolescence is a most interesting time, for although it can be trying and difficult it also presents many challenges. During this particular season of growth, many of the conditioned attitudes and patterns which may have influenced the child become more apparent in the young adult.

This period often attracts much sympathy for parents who it is felt must endure pain and hardships during their childrens' adolescence. Feelings of confusion, frustration, anger, and of being overly stressed are not solely those of the adult. The adolescent as well goes through all of these feelings,and more, as they find themselves in some cases forced by overbearing parents to remain as they were at some younger age. Being open to understanding and having empathy for the other's viewpoint, and for what they are going through, will be most helpful in reducing the "them vs. us" attitude that seems to prevail.

What makes this book different from other self-help publications on this subject is that it has been written for both parents and teens to read. Most books dealing with adolescence are directed toward the parent alone. Inasmuch as I view most parent/adolescent problems as a relationship concern, I feel that understanding what goes on, and making any attempt at improvement, needs to be a common experience. It is my hope that sharing this information will stimulate inner feelings, thoughts, and discussion, which will help develop mutual understanding.

Feelings of not being heard, projected by one's inner cry of "Why can't anyone hear me?" adds a sense of hopelessness to the pain being experienced. This cry reflects the feelings of many parents and teens who are at a loss as to which way to turn to escape the frustration and anger they feel in not being heard. There are at least two sides to every conflict situation, and when there is a mutual desire to bridge the differences that exist, it can be done. In those relationships where each one looks at and blames the other, the communicative gap grows larger and hope for resolution grows dimmer.

One of the most valuable lessons to be learned from this book is that in spite of how bad your situation may feel at times, it need not be hopeless. Without hope, the results are predictable. But, by hanging onto your faith, you may be able to create a desire and then a plan which will result in positive changes. Within the quiet and what sometimes appears as the secrecy of the young adult's mind are the same needs that we all have, to love and be loved, and be able to relate to others in a positive way.

These needs are best met by developing an atmosphere where caring, trust, and a sharing of one's feelings are experienced. This experience, so vital to creating a healthy self-image and to meaningful relationships, involves the ability to listen as well as to be heard. Therefore, opening the channels of communication is another major focus of this book. Opening these channels will enable some light to shine into those darkened areas of the mind where secret feelings and images are held, and not shared.

The format of this book, which is divided into seven parts, includes a fictional story, followed by nonfiction sections which offer guidance and points of value relating to the story. This book is non-traditional in that it speaks to two distinct age groups, parents and teens. Its objective is to create mutual understanding, and then motivate these two groups to speak to one another.

Part One contains a general view of the adolescent period, describing the dynamics of what takes place and how difficult this stage of personal growth can be. Understanding this natural process, and its effects upon all concerned, is important in dealing in a sensible manner with what takes place.

Parts Two through Five contain a story of a typical

family, much like a case study, only this study has been written in a fictional format. The story is about a family and their experiences, both good and bad, like other families with pre-teens or teens whom you might know. The purpose of this story is to provide characters and events you will be able to relate to, which will then generate thoughts and feelings to help make the discussion of your own situation easier.

The story deals with the everyday occurrences in the life of a young man named Jamie English. It could well be the drama of many young people, struggling with their self-worth and their inability to communicate with their families and friends. Jamie's thoughts will be clear to you, to help you better understand the motivation for his actions and the problems he encounters in being understood and accepted.

In exploring Jamie's self-esteem, we may better understand how many adolescents and adults feel about themselves and how these feelings affect and shape their lives. Self-esteem, the image people hold of themselves, both positive and negative, is a significant factor in motivating individual behavior and affecting interaction with others. One's self-image is developed over a period of time through personal feedback from others, especially the significant others in their lives.

Part Six contains many factors that affect how people relate to others and themselves. These subject areas have been prepared to serve as a guide for assisting in improving your relationships and minimizing your frustration.

Although this information has been developed with the parent/adolescent relationship in mind, these same principles apply to any and all relationships. The major issue when exploring and attempting to resolve parent/adolescent conflict is not the problems of the individual, but instead the problems that exist within the relationship. Adjust your thinking away from self-guilt, "what have I done wrong?" or blaming, "that terrible kid," or "my parents are just not with it," to accepting that there is a relationship problem, with dual responsibility for making changes.

Part Seven contains questions to facilitate discussion between teenagers and their parents or teachers. This discussion could lay the groundwork for increasing understanding of one another, improving communication, and in turn, moving your relationship to a better place.

The kind of environment where happiness and pain can be shared, and yet where one's need for privacy will also be respected, is indeed a supportive and healthy place to be. If some family or families can in part bridge the gap that distances them from each other through experiencing this book, then everything involved in producing it has been worthwhile.

Part One

~

A DIFFICULT SEASON
OF LIFE

UNDERSTANDING THE ADOLESCENT PERIOD

The adolescent period can be difficult for both parents and teenagers, and yet exciting as well. It is a time when important changes take place. These changes affect the physical body, where suddenly clothes are outgrown before they show wear. The sexual glands also show signs of development; in boys, their testicles mature as sperm cells begin their productive process; in girls, as their ovaries mature their menstruation cycle begins. Girls become aware of their own breast development now and boys start to shave.

Along with their physical changes, the adolescent goes through emotional and social changes as well. Parents may at this time lose sight of all the major developmental changes taking place, and their effect upon the behavior of their once sweet and obedient children. Instead, their focus is uncomfortably drawn to the emotional and behavioral transformation taking place.

As teenagers, you may be aware of how you have already begun the process of stepping forward into adulthood. This can be both a challenging and a scary experience. Even young birds, as they prepare to leave the security of their nest, are cautious and show concern about being able to fly on their own. You too may be concerned about leaving the safety of your nest, and yet a part of you is wanting to be on your own.

This transitional process is meant to be slow and natural for the adolescent, in which one foot moves forward into adulthood, while the other remains connected to the security of childhood. Patience and understanding are often fully tested during this period, as many teenagers disregard the slower trans-formation for one of changing overnight. During this more rapid change, teenagers may assertively question and challenge their parents' rules and regulations. This can also be a reactive stage for those parents and teachers who may have little tolerance for "the children" (as they may still be viewed), who no longer respond as well to direction.

Everyone in a relationship is affected by the dynamics of any person changing within the relationship. To allow for these changes, and for the prior family bond to continue, all members of the relationship must be willing to do the work required to help the relationship readjust to a balanced state. During conflict, this work is especially important.

Unfortunately, many people are fearful of conflict

and run from it instead of showing a willingness to work through it. If both parties become rigid in their demands, resolving differences can become extremely draining. When little or no change takes place, the involved parties may become frustrated and withdraw from one another, or even push each other away.

Love and hate are not opposites, as is commonly thought, rather both are high energy feeling levels. Apathy, or simply not caring what happens, is a low energy involvement. It is in this low energy state (the opposite of love) where an attempt is made at burying and ignoring hurt and angry feelings. It can be a sad time when everyone involved finds themselves regressing into childlike behavior. At that time, their actions may reflect an attitude of, "If you don't play by my rules, I won't play with you."

Parents of adolescents who withdraw during a period of conflict do nothing to resolve the bad feelings that exist. If anything, they prolong the discomfort by shutting off any possibility for meaningful relating, which may cause the negative behavior to increase. Emotional detachment, by parents from their children, causes the young people to feel unloved and unwanted. Parents too may feel unloved and rejected by adolescents who withdraw. When teenagers pull away, they often form strong connections outside their family, fully rejecting their parents.

This detachment can be dangerous for teenagers, who while feeling misunderstood and unloved, often rebel in an aggressive manner. Some turn to drugs or alcohol as the "in way" of becoming accepted by their friends. Getting high may then become their means of escaping from the world that feels so uncomfortable to them. Attempting to remove emotional pain through artificial means, such as drugs or alcohol, does nothing to resolve the difficulties that exist, and oftentimes produces even larger problems with more pain than before. Trying to eliminate pain (the symptom) without dealing with the problem (the cause), is completely ineffectual. Parents and teenagers who choose this course of action may find themselves unable to stop running from those things that need to be dealt with.

It is extremely important for those in pain, who are unable to resolve their concerns, to seek the assistance and guidance of a licensed counselor. There can be a lot of confusion caused by the mixed feelings of anger and guilt in a conflict situation. A counselor, being objective and yet empathetic, can help develop clarity on the true issues that need to be worked on.

Having mutual respect for one another makes it much easier to deal with relationship problems during this time. Mutual respect involves allowing for and valuing each other's opinions and attitudes. When respect, like love, is freely given and accepted, it becomes a valuable part of the relationship. When it is demanded and not returned, it is often lost.

The adolescent period can result in all parties "losing the war" because of their unwillingness to deal with the skirmishes. On the positive side, love and respect are strong healing agents and most parent/adolescent relationships do survive this time of conflict and growth. Firmness is required on the part of the parent, but so is love. By keeping love alive and continuing to work on improving the relationship, the odds are good that the situation will improve.

As you become more in tune with one another, (pulling together instead of apart) you may hear the other person's cry: "Why can't anyone hear me?" which parents and teens have been crying out in silence to themselves. When these cries are heard, and an attempt is made to understand them, then conflict will diminish and communications will improve. At that time, the adolescent period will be more openly accepted as a natural period of growth and change, instead of as a stage of life that is hazardous to everyone's well-being.

Part Two

∾

SUMMERTIME

Vacations and Loneliness

CHAPTER 1

~

A BOY NAMED JAMIE

The Effects of Self-esteem

Adults sometimes have difficulty in remembering back to their youth. The years tend to play tricks with memory, and after a while what has taken place in their lives becomes foggy and unclear. I suppose that's understandable with all the years gone by, and the current happenings to keep track of. But that hasn't happened to me, for I clearly remember those past years, the things that took place, and the people in my life. As I tell my story I think you may understand why my past has been important to me.

It sometimes feels as if it all just happened yesterday, and yet for me it all began about thirty years ago when I was twelve years old...

I was rather tall for my age, slender, and had more freckles than one could count. It was summertime and that was when my freckles came out in full bloom. That year it seemed they multiplied at a greater rate than usual.

I laid on my bed staring out the window at my back yard. My bed was near the window, and when I propped myself up on my pillows I could see a good part of the yard. My bedroom was my favorite place in the house. It was there that I could be alone, just me and my thoughts.

The summertime of one's life was supposed to be a glorious time (I remember reading that somewhere) especially for a boy like me. With school out and the weather just right for baseball, swimming, hide-and-seek, and all the other things kids like to do, it should have been great. But it wasn't.

My name's Jamie...Jamie English. Why anyone would have named me Jamie, especially my parents who supposedly loved me, is beyond me. I guess I shouldn't pick on them because I'm sure they loved me. Yet, of all names, why Jamie? When I have a kid, if I ever do, and if he's a boy, I'll call him Tony or Bill or John or maybe even Rocky, but definitely NOT Jamie, I thought.

Well, so much for my name, for I needed to live with it and that's all there was to it. Getting back to why summer wasn't special for me, it's a long story, but perhaps I can get to the point by introducing my family. There's Mom. She's all right I guess, but she was always telling me I should listen to and respect my elders. I'm sure she never knew what was going on inside of me, especially how I hurt. How could she know? She never listened to me, but then maybe that wasn't part of the deal. I was supposed to listen to and respect my elders, but they didn't need to listen to me.

Then there's Dad. I usually knew where I stood with him: not too well. He often told me how I didn't do most things as he expected or wanted me to. My brother George was OK, but I didn't see much of him after he left for college. I sure heard a lot about him from my folks; stuff like, "Why can't you be more like your brother George?" and, "Why don't you do as well in school as he did?" And then there's the one question that always got me, "Why is it that you don't have friends like George did?"

There were times when I hated the name George more than I did Jamie.

"Jamie, are you there?"

Whoops, that's Mom, I gotta go now. Why summertime wasn't the greatest will have to wait till later.

"Jamie, why are you in the house when it's so lovely outside?"

"I was just watching things outside through the window, and thinking — "

"Well, don't think so much and go out and play."

"Mom, I don't want — "

"Never mind, Jamie. How many times have I told you to listen to me, and to respect your elders?"

"Often, Mom."

"Then how about starting now."

"Yes, Mom. I'm going."

"Good, and don't forget to be on time for dinner. You know how Dad gets when you're not on time."

"I sure do. I'll be on time, Mom."

"That's my boy. Now go out and enjoy yourself like the rest of the children."

I thought that summer vacations were the time for being free and doing what you wanted, but that's not the way it was, at least not for me. As I walked down the street I saw the neighborhood kids playing their usual dumb games. That wasn't really the way I felt; they weren't dumb games at all.

Their games were dumb only because I wasn't involved. Why couldn't I be like other kids? Why couldn't I be like George? Whoops, it had even rubbed off on me and I was asking the same questions my parents did.

As if things weren't bad enough, I saw that terrible kid Marty from down the block coming my way. I hoped he wouldn't bug me. I did my silent prayer for insurance, but it didn't work that time.

"Hey, Jamie baby, you wanna play?" Marty asked.

"I'm busy right now, I. . .I can't," I answered quietly.

"Yeah, you're too busy. You're always too busy. Why don't you go play with yourself."

There were times like that when I just wanted to crawl into a deep cave and disappear.

I walked as fast as I could to get away from Marty and his nasty remarks. I knew exactly where I was going: to my private and secret place. Other than my room, that was my favorite hideaway. That patch of green grass surrounded by trees overlooking the lake was where I went when I wanted to be alone. I felt safe there from those things and people that bothered me. The other kids never came there; the area down by the lake was their hang out, because that's where all the girls went.

My place was everything I wanted or needed. It provided me with a place to escape to when I had to get out of the house. It was quiet and had a pretty view too, which helped me to feel good when I'd been feeling bad.

On that summer day, when Mom booted me out of the house, I went there again to be alone with my thoughts. I felt calm. There was no one to tell me how I ought to be, what I should do, or to call me names. It was just me, my inner thoughts, and my patch of grass. Sometimes when I felt very sad, I felt uncomfortable even there. On those occasions, with no one in sight, I said out loud, as if someone could hear me, "Why do I need to be so sad?" No one ever answered. I'd then ask myself, "Why can't anyone hear me?"

I had a teacher once, who I felt comfortable talking to. She would stay after school with me and we would talk about loneliness and sadness. I felt safe with her; she was different from other adults, she really listened to me. I didn't know why at the time, but Dad and Mom got upset with her; it had something to do with her suggesting that we all go to a counselor. I could still hear Dad saying to Mom, "That will be the day when I go to a shrink." In spite of how they felt about her, I enjoyed our talks. She got me to thinking that maybe I wasn't the only kid unhappy with his life. It seemed to help, feeling that I wasn't the only one, and for a short time I even felt better about myself.

I took off my shirt and laid down upon my little patch of grass. The summer breezes and the sun felt good as they gently touched my body. As I stared up at the sky, its blue space was so peaceful that I found myself drifting into a sound sleep.

Sometimes sleep felt so good, and other times it was scary because I would dream uncomfortable dreams. I once dreamt that I was in a glass enclosure, like a big cylinder. I felt that I was alone, and yet I wasn't. There were crowds of people all around staring at me and laughing. It was a frightening dream and for a while after that I was afraid to go to sleep.

This was not one of those times. When I woke up I felt good and well rested. I sat up and stretched my arms to the sky and my body swayed from side to side. I was enjoying how I felt, when all of a sudden my quiet was disturbed by a voice from behind me.

CHAPTER 2

⁓

A SCARY DREAM

Dealing with Reality

"Hi. I didn't mean to frighten you. Do you come here often?" the voice asked.

I was startled by this unexpected interruption of my space. Who was this person disturbing my privacy? I quickly put my shirt on and answered, "Hi. No, you didn't startle me."

"Well, I'm glad I didn't, but it sure looked like I did. My name's Clarence; what's yours?"

"Did you say Clarence? Gee whiz. I mean, my name's Jamie."

"I know you kinda reacted to my name. It's OK though, I'm used to it. You don't realize how lucky you are to have a neat name like Jamie."

"Do you mean that, Clarence?"

"I sure do."

With a big smile on my face I thought, "Gee, Clarence sure seems like an all right guy."

We talked for a long time. Soon our instant comfort developed into us both feeling good about each other. We found that we both went to the same school, which made it easy for us to talk about many of the kids who we knew, at least by reputation. We agreed on those we thought were OK and also about those who we weren't wild about. We even shared how we felt about being left out of school activities. All of a sudden I realized that a lot of time had passed, what with my nap and all of our talking. I looked at my watch and was surprised to see what time it was. I realized that I was going to be late for dinner.

"I gotta go now, Clarence, but I'd sure like to see you again."

"Me too. Let's plan on it, Jamie."

We exchanged telephone numbers and climbed down the rocks together. This was the first friend I could remember feeling that good about. I wouldn't mind sharing my private place with Clarence, I thought. As I ran home, my good feelings about myself and my new friend stayed with me. I ran by the street where Marty was still playing ball and he again called out to me, "Where you running, Jamie baby?"

"None of your business, Marty." I replied.

I could see Marty's look of shock at my unusual response. As a matter of fact, I even surprised myself. I was excited at being able to give that bully some of his own medicine. Even though I felt good about what I said, I was also concerned about how he might react, so I ran faster till I was past his block. Unfortunately, my good feelings didn't last very long. As I entered the house, there stood my mother and father looking angry as they awaited my arrival.

"Jamie, what did I tell you about being home on time for

dinner?" my mother said.

"Let me handle this, dear," my father interrupted. "You know, Jamie, that eating meals together is a very important time for us. It's that time of day when we as a family come together."

"I know Dad, and I'm sorry I'm late, but I've got a good reason." I tried as best I could to get my two cents in.

"You always have good excuses son, but they're never quite good enough."

"But, Dad — "

"Jamie, how many times have I told you not to interrupt when your father or I are speaking?"

It's no use, I thought. I would like to tell them about Clarence, but when the two of them gang up on me I might as well retreat or surrender.

"Perhaps the best way for you to learn, young man, is to go to your room without dinner."

"But, Dad — "

"I mean now, Jamie."

"Yes, Dad."

I marched off to my room, with the smell of Mom's cooking lingering strongly behind me. I breathed deeply, holding the smells within me, as if I were a condemned man who had just missed his last meal. It would be easier if she wasn't such a good cook, I thought. All memories of my good time with my new friend were leaving me; instead my thoughts and feelings turned to sadness again.

While I sat in the loneliness of my room feeling sorry for myself and questioning how unfair my life was, my parents, who were preparing to fill their stomachs, did some questioning of their own.

"Why do you suppose he has so much difficulty in being on time for dinner?" Dad asked.

"It's not only his being late, Fred, there's much more involved than that. I don't think he's a happy child; frankly speaking, I'm concerned." Mom even looked concerned.

"I never quite thought of it in that light, I mean that there's a problem that we need to be concerned about. I know he isn't like George, but then my brother and I were not exactly alike either," Dad replied.

"Do you suppose, Fred, that that's part of his problem? I mean, that perhaps it's partially created by us, when we compare him with George, and other things that we say?" Mom asked.

"Hey now, just wait a minute, Janet," Dad answered, "I can just see you developing a good case of the guilts; why do we need to be the bad guys in this scenario?"

Mom replied quickly, "Do there need to be good guys and bad guys? I'm not talking about a TV drama, I'm referring to our son; and if he's having problems, and if by chance we're contributing to whatever is bothering him, shouldn't we talk about it?"

"I know what's going on with you, you're upset because I sent him to his room without dinner. As far as I'm concerned, you can bring him some food if that's going to make you feel better, but I'm hungry and tired. It's been a long day and I would just as well put off this discussion till later."

"There just never seems to be a good time for us to talk about Jamie. Well, I'll tell you, Fred, we are his parents and we need to find time to talk about this. I will fix your dinner and then I'll bring Jamie's dinner to his room. I want you to know that I realize this is an uncomfortable subject for you, but it's one we both need to deal with for the sake of our son."

"Hey, I love Jamie too. It's just that this is not the best time for us to get into a lengthy discussion. After all, I'm tired. It was a long, rough day and I'm hungry."

While my parents were making their first effort at recognizing that a problem existed, I once again felt alone and sad. I sat at the window staring out at the street which was now empty and dark, and I also thought of myself as being empty and dark. Why do I need to be like I am? Why can't I be more like the other kids, even like Marty. Those thoughts kept going through my mind. Why, oh why, can't Mom and Dad love me like they love George? The more I questioned, the sadder I became.

To escape from my sadness, I stretched out on my bed and dozed off. Once again, I entered my dream world. I dreamt that I was involved in an adventure on the high seas. I was tied and bound aboard this large schooner, sitting in the hold of the ship, cold and hungry. It was dark and I was unable to cover myself because my hands were tightly bound. I was completely helpless. There were rats in the hold busily eating their meals, which consisted of the largest chunk of cheese I had ever seen. Suddenly, the doors above me opened and the brightness of the light blinded me for a few moments. When I was able to see again, a number of pirates were coming down into the hold. They grabbed me and pulled me towards the opening. The frightened rats left their cheese and scurried away as I was dragged past them. Their cheese smelled better than any I had ever smelled before. Once on deck I saw this mean looking pirate with a patch over his eye, who the others referred to as Marty the Terrible, coming towards me.

"Well, Jamie baby," the mean pirate yelled out at me, "your time has come me bucko. You have chosen not to play on our terms, so now you die."

The pirates placed me on the plank and poked me with their swords, forcing me to hobble towards the edge, where I could see the ocean splashing below me. Fierce sharks jumped out of the water as if anxiously awaiting their next meal, which in this case, unfortunately for me, was to be a Jamie burger without the bun. The pirate chief, Marty the Terrible, came towards me, sword in hand, forcing me to walk to the end of the plank. As I stepped backwards I closed my eyes, unable to face my fate. I felt myself falling, that awful feeling of falling through space into the nothingness that separated me from those hungry sharks. Just as I was about to hit the water, I felt a pair of hands reach out, as if from nowhere, clutching me away from danger.

I woke up with Mom holding me in her arms. "Jamie, you were dreaming," she whispered softly to me. "Everything is OK."

"Oh thanks, Mom, you saved me. It was awful; they were going to eat me."

"Nobody is going to eat you, dear. It was all a dream," she said reassuringly. As Mom held me close, she heard me sob. She too began to cry and we comforted each other. We realized that it had been too long since we last hugged like that. We continued to hold each other and to enjoy our good feelings.

It seemed like many hours passed; I ate the dinner that Mom had brought me and we talked endlessly. Mom did a lot of listening, which was most unusual. It was good being close, and best of all, I finally felt that I had been heard. Not once did I hear her say anything about respecting my elders.

When I woke up the next morning, the sun was shining into my room and the birds on the tree just outside my window were singing their own special songs to each other. What a beautiful day it was. I raised my arms above my head and stretched as far as I could, removing the sleep from my body. Yes, that was the start of a beautiful summer day.

As the days and weeks of summer passed, my friendship with Clarence continued to grow. We spent our time together sharing the patch of grass among the rocks. On a few occasions we even went down to the lake where we swam and admired some of the pretty girls who seemed to spend all their time sunning themselves.

Throughout the remaining weeks of summer vacation I was careful not to be late for dinner again, which helped keep me out of trouble with my parents.

My summer got better after meeting Clarence and with my continuing closeness with Mom. However, I was aware that Mom and Dad were arguing a lot more. Those arguments, which stopped abruptly when I entered the room, left me wondering if I was the cause of their fights. Alone in my room, I thought about my father and I questioned whether he loved me or not. I missed being close with him and hoped that one day the two of us might talk so that I could tell him how much I loved him.

At the end of summer, George came home for a week. It was a nice time for us all, with the whole family together again. We spent a lot of time together, George and I. He told me of his experiences in college, his girl friend, and his job. I was sad when he left to return to school. I could tell that Mom and Dad were sad too, for it was the first time I ever saw Dad cry. I couldn't help feeling what they felt and I cried too.

I will remember that summer and the meaningful things that happened. As far as summers go, it was better than usual. But that was behind me, for in a few days I'd be entering a new school, and with those thoughts in mind I felt excited and concerned about how I would fit in.

Looking out my window, I saw the first leaves of fall floating down from the branches of the tall oak tree in our back yard. Mother Nature reminded me that summer was over.

Part Three

∾

AUTUMN

New Beginnings

CHAPTER 3

~

SCRUBS AND JUNIOR HIGH

Adjusting to Change

Autumn was a nice time of the year. The trees began to change their colors and the summer's heat and humidity gave way to the gentle breezes of fall.

I woke up well before my alarm went off, which was unusual for me, as I have been known to enjoy my sleep. But that morning was special; it was my first day in junior high. I hadn't slept too well the night before. I kept thinking about the new school and what it would be like. It felt strange that I was going to junior high. As I dressed, I thought to myself that one day I'm a graduating senior, and then the next I'm back at the beginning again. To have said that I was nervous was the understatement of the year. George used to tell of the pressures kids felt at exam time. It didn't make much sense to me then, but it did now, and I wasn't even taking any tests.

Mom insisted that I eat a good breakfast, so that I would

have more energy and be able to think better. Far be it from me to question her beliefs on the subject. However, I knew by the way I felt, that if I put anything into my stomach it was going to come right back up. We compromised, I ate a little and I kept it down.

The time had come for me to face it. I couldn't think of any way out of it, so I took my new notebook and pencils, said my goodbyes to Mom and Dad, and off I went. There was no more walking across the street as I had been able to do in elementary school. Instead I had to take a bus to get to my new school.

The bus stop was crowded. It seemed like everyone going to this school came from my neighborhood. As I watched, it was easy to tell which kids were new to the school, like me. We looked frightened, while the others laughed and fooled around. I couldn't help feeling like they were staring and laughing at me. Then I saw someone I recognized from my old school: Marty the bully. I couldn't believe it, even he looked scared. He didn't say a word to anyone. He just clung to his notebook, holding it tightly to his chest, as if he were shielding himself from the enemy. I was happy to see the bus finally arrive. At that point I was willing to do anything to get away from that crowd. I wiggled my way onto the bus; keeping one eye on Marty I moved as far as I could from where he sat. When we arrived at school I waited while the others pushed their way out, and then I got off.

The halls of Farnsworth Junior High were crowded with kids going in all directions. It was sure different from my old school, I thought, as I was bumped from side to side. The confusion was overwhelming and yet I remembered my dad's advice to me, "Jamie, there are bound to be situations on your first day that may be scary to you, but don't panic." I wondered at the time how anyone could stop panicking when feeling panicky, but I chose not to get into it any deeper.

All new seventh graders were told to report to the auditorium. Not knowing where it was, added to my confusion, so I decided to ask. Smart thing to do. Right? No, wrong. I stopped two kids walking in my direction and asked, "Excuse me, could you tell me where the auditorium is?"

Their response was deafening as they shouted at the top of their lungs, "Scrub! Scrub! Scrub!"

I thought they would never stop; how embarrassing. It felt like everyone in the school was staring and laughing at me. "Don't panic, don't panic," I kept repeating to myself. I was about to run, where to I don't know, when all of a sudden a girl grabbed my arm and said, "I'm going that way, I'll show you where it is."

Saved from a doom worse then death, I thought. I wished that we could walk faster to get away from the echoing sound of that terrible word "scrub," which still rang in my ears.

"Thanks, I just didn't know where it was," I said.

"Yes I know, and those kids weren't too helpful, to say the least. By the way, my name's Diane; what's yours?"

"My name's Jamie," I told her as softly as I could.

"Did you say Tony?"

"No."

"Well then, what is it?"

"Jamie," I said louder.

"Oh, glad to meet you, Jamie."

"Me, too, Diane. I mean I'm also glad to meet you."

I thought Diane was the friendliest person at Farnsworth and also the prettiest. Her hair was long and blonde and she

51

had the bluest eyes I'd ever seen. I wondered why this pretty girl was helping me.

We arrived at the auditorium. I could hear myself saying thanks under my breath as I sighed with relief that we were there. I had gotten through my first panic and had survived it, thanks to Diane.

The auditorium was crowded with kids all talking at the same time. Their chorus of voices blending together reminded me of the sounds I once heard on a family trip to New York. Standing under the Brooklyn Bridge the cars overhead made their own kind of music, a continuous humming sound as the wheels made contact with the steel grating.

As we entered the auditorium, Diane waved to some friends who were calling her to join them. So we said our goodbyes and I managed to catch her glance long enough to say thanks again. She nodded and I knew she understood how much I appreciated her help.

I was on my own in this sea of humanity, with no friends to beckon me. I found an empty seat which allowed me to blend in with the others. I stayed there until after the opening remarks by Dr. Goodson, the principal, and the orientation which followed. We were told what was expected of us as new students, and were given class schedules and instructions on how to find our homeroom. I noticed Marty, still clutching his notebook tightly. I was amazed. He looked as frightened as I felt. But that couldn't be, not Marty the bully. I had never seen him frightened of anything or anybody.

Before leaving the auditorium I looked for Clarence, but couldn't find him. Being worried about getting to class on time, especially on the first day, I gave up my search and rushed down the hall, room map in hand.

My homeroom teacher, Miss Richards, stood in front of the room as I entered. I waited, wondering if she was going to assign me a seat. I didn't need to wonder for long, for with a gesture of her pointer I knew I was to take any seat. She then indicated that the seats we selected would be permanent for the remainder of the term, unless our behavior made it necessary for her to make a change. I went to the very last row, seating myself where I felt I would be safely out of sight.

I saw Marty enter the room. Of all people, why did he need to be in my homeroom? I looked away so as not to catch his attention, thinking that if I didn't look at him maybe he wouldn't see me. There wasn't much logic to that, but sometimes it worked. That wasn't one of my better days, for out of the corner of my eye I saw Marty approach the back row; he sat down in the seat right next to mine. I couldn't believe my luck.

"Hi, Jamie, how're you doing?" he asked, more quietly than I had heard him speak before.

"Oh, OK, Marty. How are you doing?" I replied.

At that moment we were both startled by the sound of the teacher's voice, "There will be no talking in this room, please."

I felt she had to be talking to us. Both Marty and I responded at the same time, as if we had been rehearsing our lines and cues, "Yes ma'am, Miss Richards," we shouted loud and clear.

The class started to snicker. Marty and I looked at the empty space above us, acting as if we were invisible.

"That will be enough," Miss Richards informed the class in a firm tone, and the class responded with respectful silence.

At lunch time Marty suggested that we eat together. Having spent the morning sitting next to him helped me feel more comfortable with him. Besides, there didn't seem to be any easy way out of it, so I agreed.

The caf was loaded with kids. I looked for Clarence and Diane, and not being able to spot them, I decided to relax as best I could and enjoy my lunch.

Marty was quite talkative. I couldn't understand how he managed to eat all his lunch and still find time to talk non-stop. My suspicion seemed to be right. This guy, who I thought was always so sure of himself, was as frightened as I was on our first day in junior high. We sort of became school buddies, Marty and I. At least for the time being it felt OK for me to hang out with him at school. I thought of it more as a matter of survival than anything else; I figured that two was better than one in the kind of a situation we were in. When they called us "scrubs" again it felt less scary when it applied to both of us instead of only me.

As time went on I became more at ease at Farnsworth. There were a few things that took me a little longer to get used to. One was remembering the combination for my locker and the other was taking showers with a bunch of guys in gym class. I don't believe I'll ever live down my first shower experience. Physical Education, or P.E. as we called it, also included taking showers every day. Nobody told me that I wasn't supposed to wear my bathing suit into the shower. That was the first and last time I did that. I learned the hard way, when the other kids laughed me right back into the locker room. As sensitive as I was about showing my private parts in public, I soon became a nudie like the rest of the gang. Well, not exactly. I still didn't like it, but I did it anyway.

As soon as I got home that first day I called Clarence. His father answered, telling me Clarence wasn't able to speak to me. I tried to find out why he wasn't in school, but all I got was a strange response without any details. I felt something was wrong and yet I had no idea what it could be. I found myself becoming concerned about him and yet there was nothing I could do except to call him again the next day.

School became more bearable as time went on, and even Miss Richards was less scary to me. I still knew that she meant business when she said what she wanted, but there was a light and caring side to her as well. It didn't take long for me to know that I liked her. Another of my new experiences in junior high was having different teachers for various subjects. Getting along with all my new teachers, instead of one, and rushing from class to class trying not to be late was a pain. As I became more comfortable with Miss Richards, I wished that I could have her for all my classes, instead of just homeroom and English. There was nothing I could do about it, so I accepted it.

Dad always said, "You can pick your friends, but you can't pick your relatives and your bosses." I could have added teachers to that, and covered all the bases. Mom told me that Dad was quite a philosopher. I'm not too sure what she meant by that, but since I couldn't understand many of Dad's little sayings, I figured maybe that's what being a philosopher was all about.

Life at home stayed pretty much the same. Mom and Dad were still at it. They argued a lot and it was scary to me at times. If they had no time for me before, they had even less now. Sometimes I heard Mom crying after their fights. Even in my room, I could hear their arguing. When this happened,

I buried my head in my pillow and hoped that it was all a bad dream and that when I woke up everything would be OK.

CHAPTER 4

~

MYSTERY INVOLVING CLARENCE

Can You Escape From Life?

After having tried several times without any luck to reach Clarence, I became concerned. I was ready to go to his house to find out what was going on with him, when Mr. Stewart, Clarence's father, called. He asked me to come over to their house after school that day. He said he wanted to talk to me about Clarence. I felt somewhat frightened and yet I wanted to know where Clarence had been and what was wrong. I told Mom about Mr. Stewart's call and that I might be a little late coming home. When I got to Clarence's house, his mother greeted me, "Hello, Jamie, I'm so glad to see you. Won't you please come in."

"Hi, Mrs. Stewart. Where's Clarence. Is he OK?"

"That's what we want to talk to you about. Please come in and we'll explain."

As I entered the house, it seemed quite different being

there without Clarence and his friendly smile. Mr. Stewart was at home, which also struck me as strange, considering that I never saw him there so early. Clarence had made a point of telling me that he hardly ever had dinner with his father because he usually came home so late. Mr. Stewart motioned for me to sit on the couch; I sat down and they both joined me. I felt it best in this case to heed Mom's words about remaining silent until spoken to. Mr. Stewart spoke first, "Jamie, I'm glad you were able to come over. Mrs. Stewart and I want to ask you some questions about Clarence. We know that the two of you have become very close this last summer and I . . . that is we thought perhaps you could shed a little light on certain things that have us puzzled."

"I'd be glad to help in any way I can, Mr. Stewart, but can't you tell me what's wrong?" I asked.

"Yes, dear," Mrs. Stewart said to her husband, "we need to tell Jamie what has happened."

I was glad I'd finally find out what happened to Clarence. The suspense of not knowing was just too much for me, yet, I was also frightened of what I might hear. Mr. Stewart looked sad. He stared at the floor as if he was trying to decide whether to share the information with me or not. The silence seemed endless. Finally he spoke, "You may be wondering why I'm finding it so difficult to tell you what's wrong. Well, it's just that it's hard for me to say that Clarence tried to take his life."

I couldn't believe what I heard. Not Clarence! Of all people, not Clarence. I wanted to cry or shout, but I couldn't. Instead I blurted out, "What happened? I mean, I mean, I just don't understand."

"We know how you feel, because we can't understand it

59

either." Mr. Stewart said as he began to sob.

Mrs. Stewart put her hand on her husband's shoulder to comfort him as she continued to explain, "We wanted to talk to you, Jamie, because we thought you might know what bothered Clarence and caused him to do something like that." Without hesitation she added, "Clarence swallowed a large number of my sleeping pills."

"Oh my God, I just can't believe it, not Clarence," I repeated. "How is he?" I quickly added.

"He's upstairs resting. He can't see anyone right now, but he's doing much better. For a while it was touch and go as to whether he'd make it." She found it difficult to tell me this.

"It's still so hard to believe," I said.

"Getting back to why we asked you here, do you have any idea as to what might have caused him to do what he did?" Mr. Stewart asked.

"No, sir, at least I don't think so. I just saw him last week."

"Was he angry at us, or is there anything else that you can remember?"

Mr. Stewart's questions came so fast that I couldn't think.

"I really don't know, I mean we talked a lot when we got together, but it wasn't anything special. I mean, nothing that would have made Clarence do something like that."

"Just think for a moment, Jamie; did he seem very sad?" Clarence's mother asked.

"Well, yes, Clarence was sad and feeling a lot of pressure, but that's not unusual. I mean, who doesn't feel like that at times." We talked for what seemed like a long time. They continued to question me, but I didn't feel like they were blaming me. It was more like they were panicky and needing to find answers. There was no question about it, they were upset, but then so was I. I told them that I would think more about what went on with Clarence and me, before he — I, too, found it difficult to say that my good friend, gentle and kind Clarence, O.D.'d on pills.

Walking home, I kept going over in my mind what Clarence had said to me that might have been a clue to what he was thinking of doing. I kept reviewing and reliving our last conversations, but being so upset I couldn't think straight.

The Stewarts had already called Mom and Dad. So by the time I got home they knew what had happened and were waiting for me. Mom threw her arms around me and held me close. I began to cry; my tears and feelings flowed freely. Dad also did his best to comfort me. Yet, his need to be the advice giving philosopher, always on top of things, stood in the way. At that moment I wanted so much for us to be close, and for him to love me. Instead, he insisted on saying that this kind of thing could not happen in our family.

I wanted to shake Dad and warn him that it could happen to any one of us, especially me. Somewhere hidden within my fears, I knew the truth; for on a few occasions, in the depth of my own sadness, I too had wondered if life was worth living. I wished that I could tell Dad about all those feelings I'd had, but I didn't think he'd understand. Fortunately, those feelings were never stronger than my hope that with time things would get better. When I felt that bad, it helped to imagine myself being married and having a family of my own and all of us loving each other.

When I was finally allowed to visit Clarence, I wondered what it was going to be like for us. I had been warned by his parents to be careful about what and how much I said about his "accident," as they referred to it. I understood their concern about possibly upsetting him. Yet I was worried about what to say to my friend who had just tried to end his life, not to mention how we could even carry on a conversation when there were so many things that couldn't be talked about. I hoped that we wouldn't be too uncomfortable. As I entered his room he sat up in bed and smiled at me. We greeted each other warmly and I realized that our friendship was much stronger than anything else. I knew that all I wanted was to be supportive to him. It took a few moments

for us to find the right words to say to each other. He was obviously feeling some embarrassment about what he'd done. We soon got past that and were back to being our usual selves.

After visiting for a while, Clarence told me that it was still scary for him to talk about what he did. I felt good that he was able to say that to me. I assured him that when the time was right it would be OK for us to rap, and that I had no great need for us to talk about it now. However, what I said wasn't entirely true. There was so much I wanted to know, yet I knew I needed to respect his wishes. Clarence did mention that he and his family were seeing a therapist who was helping them to understand the situation and to communicate with each other. Clarence and I had a lot more in common than either of us had realized.

Knowing that I shouldn't stay too long and that I had to get home for dinner, I quickly brought Clarence up to date on everything that was happening at school. I told him about Marty, Diane, and Miss Richards, and I promised him that I would come back the next day. I left feeling good about having seen my friend, even though I still had many questions about his "accident."

In the quiet of my room, as I thought about Clarence, I tried desperately to figure it out, but the same questions without answers kept repeating themselves. I thought about how he must have been hurting and neither his parents nor I had any idea what was going on with him. I felt a little guilty, as if I should have known, and then maybe I could have talked him out of it. Yet I knew that in spite of our closeness, there were many personal things that I couldn't share with him. With us being so much alike, I understood his being unable to talk about what was going on with him before he took those pills.

The more I thought about what Dad had said, the angrier I became. His attitude of passing the situation off with, "It couldn't happen in our family," was like saying everybody else's family had problems, but not ours. Where had he been hiding? Didn't he realize how much I'd been hurting and how frightened I got when he and Mom yelled at each other? Other kids would say, "What can you expect from parents?" but that just didn't cut it with me.

I needed Mom and Dad to want me and to love me. I thought how I would have given anything to have Dad just put his arms around me and tell me that he loved me. I wasn't willing to write them off with a "what can you expect from parents attitude." Maybe it's true, that I expected too much from them. Perhaps a kid was supposed to know that his parents loved him, instead of waiting for them to tell him so. Yet, I thought that if they loved me, why was it so hard for them to just say it once in a while? If I were worthwhile, maybe it would have been easier for them. It was all so confusing. As I relived all that was going on with me, I again felt unhappy with myself and my life.

Laying on my bed, I wished I could have slept, and then I wouldn't have had to think about my parents and Clarence and all the other things that bothered me. The pressure was becoming too much for me and I wanted to escape from it all. Oh my God! Could that have been what went on with Clarence, that he just wanted to sleep and to remove those unhappy thoughts that were always in his mind? It all seemed to make sense. Except that the answer was not one that I liked very much. Although I felt better having some understanding of

Clarence, the frightening part was knowing how closely this applied to me. It's scary, because too often I felt as I was feeling at that moment: wishing that I could escape from everything and everybody.

At least it seemed a little clearer to me why kids like Clarence, or even I, do crazy things like ending it all. If only he could have talked to someone first, like his parents, or me. I realized that saying over and over what he should have done wasn't helping him. Yet, maybe it helped me, for I made a promise to myself that night: before I would ever consider doing anything like what Clarence did, I would talk to my parents, and if they didn't listen I'd find someone who would. I hadn't done much praying in a while, but I did pray that night that things would get better for us all.

CHAPTER 5

∾

JAMIE'S FIRST DATE

Boys and Girls Relating

School started off great that following day. Diane asked if I wanted to join her for lunch. Can you imagine, Diane asking me to join her? Excited and frightened, I blurted out "yes" before she had time to complete her question. When am I going to stop doing these embarrassing things? But then, as Dad often said, "Son, don't ever argue with success, enjoy it."

In that situation, it made sense to me, and I said to myself, "Jamie don't fight it, something good is happening to you." I decided to stay with the good feelings I was having, and waited patiently for lunch time. Wouldn't you know it, Marty did a whole trip on me about why I wasn't having lunch with him. As soon as he let me get a word in I told him, "It's because I'm having lunch with Diane, that's why." If anything was to set him off, that did; he ribbed me the rest of the morning about my loving Diane. Very often the old

Marty reappeared, and then there was no living with him. I didn't care. The important thing was that Diane and I were having lunch together. I wouldn't have dared to tell anyone, especially Marty, that up to then I never had lunch with a girl before. I kept repeating to myself, "This is like my first real date, a date with Diane, wow!"

When the bell rang for lunch I was out of my mind with excitement about spending time with Diane. Rushing to the caf, I got there before anyone else. I stood at the entrance and waited for Diane to arrive. Maybe I overdid it, being so anxious, but beating the whole school to the caf was another first for me. Marty walked by holding his hand over his mouth snickering. Between his snickers he mumbled, "Jamie loves Diane." He kept repeating it in kind of a musical chant, like only Marty could.

I felt kind of strange standing there in front of the caf looking at everyone as they entered, and them looking at me. Diane finally arrived, looking cute as could be. Her blonde hair seemed to be blonder than usual, and her blue eyes, I hadn't remembered them being that blue. There was no two ways about it, she was the most beautiful girl at Farnsworth and there she was about to have lunch with me.

I can't remember what I ate for lunch that day, but I won't forget how good I felt sitting with her. I had trouble remembering what she said, as my mind drifted from our conversation to her beautiful blue eyes. Maybe Marty was right, maybe the feelings I was having are what love is all about. Could it be, could I be in love with Diane?

Diane told me that she had an extremely important question that only I could answer. I wondered what it was that could only be asked of me. My thoughts went from one possibility to another. Could it be that she was going to ask me if I wanted to go steady, or something like that? I wondered.

Within the few seconds that passed, many possible questions came to mind and I rehearsed some answers. Then she finally asked her big question, "Jamie, as a boy, I need to ask you something very important. How do you feel about girls wearing braces?"

"Wearing what?" I said.

"Braces. Certainly you know what braces are?" she asked.

"Oh sure, braces. Of course I know what braces are. I mean everybody knows what braces are."

"Well, what do you think? Do you think I would look OK with braces?"

I couldn't believe her question. I thought for sure she was going to ask about us. I tried as hard as I could to play it cool. So I quickly got myself back together and answered her question, "You'd look fantastic in braces, Diane."

"Do you really think so, Jamie? I mean, you think it would be OK?"

"Diane, I hope I don't upset you by what I'm going to say, but you'd look great in anything."

"Thank you, Jamie, and of course I'm not upset. How could I be upset with you when you say such nice things to me."

"Diane, I want to say something else to you. I'll never forget how kind you were to me the first day of school — "

"You don't need to thank me, Jamie. Those kids were just a bunch of nerds, with a capital N."

"Diane, oh Diane..."

"Yes, Jamie?"

"Diane, I like you; I mean I like you a lot."

"I know, Jamie, and I like you, too. A lot."

The bell rang, telling us that lunch was over. The timing couldn't have been better, because I don't know what I could've said after that. I floated back to class, feeling better than I ever remember. Can you imagine, the most beautiful girl at Farnsworth telling me she liked me, too. I mean me, of all people? Then all of a sudden I remembered Marty, and thought that I mustn't walk into the room with a big smile on my face. I must have overdone it playing it cool, because Marty took one look at me and remarked, "Gee, did it go that bad?"

"No," I replied.

"Well, then tell me what happened," he said.

"Nothin' happened. Does something always need to happen when friends get together?" I felt myself getting angry at Marty's questioning

"You know what I mean. What did the two of you talk about?" Marty asked impatiently.

"It was just about school stuff, that's all." I didn't want to continue to be questioned about Diane and me.

"Oh, how boring." Marty recognized that our conversation was going nowhere. He opened his book and waited for class to begin.

I felt relieved that his questioning was over. I allowed my mind to return to nice thoughts of Diane. All I could think about was how neat she was and how I had been able to tell her that I liked her. More importantly, I remembered her saying, "And I like you, a lot, too."

What we said to each other kept repeating itself in my mind, until all of a sudden I was startled by Miss Richards' voice, "Jamie, how many times must I repeat myself?"

My gosh, I'd done it again. All of the kids in the class were staring at me, and Marty snickered.

"Only once more, Miss Richards," I quickly replied, trying desperately to understand what she was talking about. This time the whole class laughed out loud. There was no question about it, I had said the wrong thing again.

"Jamie, as a special homework assignment, I want you to write a paragraph on the subject of 'The Importance of Paying Attention in Class.' Futhermore, you will read this report to the entire class tomorrow. Is that understood?" Miss Richards asked in a stern voice.

"Yes, ma'am, I will. I mean, I do." I wondered why I kept

doing that to myself.

When school ended that day, it was none too soon for me. I went home thinking that I would write her dumb paragraph and I would make a fool of myself again reading it to the class. But none of that could take away from the great feelings I had about Diane and my first date with her.

"The Importance of Paying Attention in Class," I'm sure wasn't remembered as a literary masterpiece. However, neither was it something that Miss Richards' class or I easily forgot. I guess I did OK with it until I got to the end. It was during that part of my writing assignment that I remembered what Dad advised regarding being a good salesman, and the need for making a strong closing statement. He said, "When completing your sale, sum up all the strong points in a neat package and then always ask for the order."

There was no question in my mind that Dad was a good salesman, so I listened to his advice and I closed my assignment by asking for the order, so to speak. It read: "In closing, I hope that I have given you all the important points on why I should pay attention in class. Now I would like to ask something of you, and that is, because I know how important it is and you now know how important it is, please don't ask me any questions until you're sure that you have my complete attention, which will save me needing to do this again. I thank you all for giving me your attention."

At least this time when the class laughed, Miss Richards joined in with them, which made me feel I did OK with it. After all, she couldn't have been that angry if she was that happy.

I was glad when Clarence returned to school. Marty, as always, was curious and wanted to know why Clarence didn't start school with the rest of us. Clarence played it cool with him and the others. His standard response to those who were curious was: "I had a bad case of the flu." I agreed with him that at times a little white lie was the right answer, considering the situation.

We spent a lot of time together, Clarence and I. After a while it became easier for him to share with me about what had happened to him. I was concerned how similar his situation at home was to mine. At the same time, how he reacted to his problems and what caused him to take those pills gave me a lot to think about. He told me he wasn't trying to take his life. Although those thoughts had entered his mind, he said his purpose was mainly to let his parents know that he needed their attention. We agreed with his therapist's statement, "There are better ways to get attention than by hurting yourself." Clarence made it clear that he would never do anything like that again. I could tell by how he looked and what he said that he meant it.

CHAPTER 6

~

A MAJOR EMOTIONAL EVENT

Divorce and Guilt

Clarence and I got together one afternoon after he had met Diane. He agreed with everything I had said about her. He went on and on about how lucky I was, and how special she was. He emphasized his feelings by saying, "She sure is a babe." Fortunately, Diane also took an immediate liking to Clarence, so the three of us became the best of buddies. When Clarence and I were alone, we talked about our future as adults, and what it would be like. In my fantasy I always included Diane. After what Clarence had been through, it was important for him to have thoughts of better tomorrows.

Having enjoyed my time with Clarence, I went home feeling good about our friendship and the great times we were having together. Unfortunately, my good feelings didn't last very long. As soon as I walked into the house, Mom and Dad asked me to join them. They told me that they had something important to discuss. Not liking the sound of their serious tone, I wanted to say that if it's bad news, count me out. I felt that I'd had enough to last me and I didn't want any more. But knowing better, I didn't say anything. Instead, I did as they asked. With my chest throbbing with nervousness, I sat down and waited to hear what they had to say. I could tell by the way they looked and acted that something serious had happened.

Both Mom and Dad looked more upset than I had seen before. They stared at each other, as if wondering who would be the first to talk. I almost did, just to break the ice. Whatever it was, they would have to kick it off themselves. So I waited for what seemed like the longest time.

Dad finally took the first step, "Jamie, there's something important that we need to talk to you about. It's not easy for your mother or me, but it's something that we all need to discuss."

I thought to myself, "Please, get to the point. Have I messed up again, or is someone sick, or are we going to move?" I didn't want to move now that I had Clarence and Diane and I would miss Marty, too, now that I'd learned to exist with him. My mind flipped to George. That's what it must be; something has happened to George. My thoughts were interrupted by Mom, who continued where Dad left off.

"Jamie, what Dad and I want to tell you, is that sometimes mothers and fathers go through changes in their lives that affect the whole family. What I'm trying to say, Jamie, is that as you may know your dad and I have not been getting along too well lately. You've been aware, I'm sure, of our discussions, which neither of us have wanted to bother you with."

"What's going on? I don't understand," I cried out. The

truth of the matter was that I did understand, but I didn't want to hear it. What Mom had called "discussions" were more like battles; but this was not the time to correct her.

"Jamie, you're not a child anymore, and we feel you should know the truth. We know you're going to feel hurt for a while, but it's not as bad as it may sound," Dad added.

"What your father and I want you to know is that we're going to separate for a while. It doesn't mean forever. It means that he will get an apartment of his own until we both have had time to work things out."

I started to cry. I didn't want to, but I couldn't help myself. The tears continued as I thought that I had caused it. I felt it was something I had done. As they both tried to comfort me, I couldn't help blurting out, "I know it's my fault, but I'm willing to change. I'll do anything. I promise I will."

"It's nothing you've done, son; it's just that we need time alone for a while to think things out," Dad said.

At this point it didn't matter what they said; I felt I was losing my family and that I had caused it. I could tell that Dad was uncomfortable with how I was reacting. He couldn't hide his sadness, which showed in the way he kept staring at the living room floor. There was nothing more that any of us could say that hadn't been said. Finally, in a quiet voice unlike his normal tone, Dad said, "I need to go now." He gathered some of his clothes into a suitcase, put them in his car and was gone. I don't think I'll ever forget how I felt seeing him drive off, while Mom and I stood there crying. The one person I needed so badly was gone and the pain I felt was unbearable.

It was pretty gloomy around the house in the days that followed. We tried to cheer each other up, but neither Mom nor I were successful at it. When we talked, Mom kept trying to convince me that I wasn't the cause of their breakup. As hard as she tried, I still wasn't able to accept what she said. I had made up my mind that I was to blame, and I couldn't see any other possibility.

A few weeks later, the situation hadn't changed much, except that Dad had invited me to visit him at his new place. I was excited, and when I arrived I explored every inch of his living quarters. He had a furnished one room apartment, with a bed that came out of the wall, which impressed me. Imagine a bed that he called Murphy, which hid in a wall. I

continued to visit Dad often, and became comfortable in his small home away from home.

Dad and I had difficulty at first finding things to talk about. It seemed strange, having lived with him all my life, and yet here we were, not knowing what to say to each other. To ease our discomfort, we did a lot of going places and doing things, like going out to eat, and to movies. One time we even went to the park where we played ball. It had been a long time since the two of us had done that. It was great being alone with Dad and doing things together.

Mom evidently had been talking to Dad, for he questioned me a lot about my feelings of guilt. For the most part he threw a lot of "why" questions at me, which I didn't have any answers for. I told him that I was feeling bad about having caused their separation, but in spite of Dad's insistence that it wasn't my fault, which was no different than what I was getting from Mom, I still continued to feel that it was. I could tell that he was becoming frustrated with my inability to see it his way. However, what was I supposed to do? I felt it was my fault and I couldn't change those feelings, no matter what he or Mom said.

The passing of time supposedly makes bad experiences easier to accept, but for me it didn't seem to work that way. On the positive side I was still seeing Dad, which made me happy. But it was still hard to accept that Mom and Dad were not living together. Even my grades at school dropped. I just couldn't keep up my interest, not with all those things going on in my life. I never was what might be considered a great student, even under normal circumstances, and this was far from normal. I had managed to get my share of B's and C's, but never failing grades as I was now. My behavior grades were also taking a nose dive.

One day Miss Richards asked that I stay after school to discuss my grades. Not her, too, I thought. I didn't need her getting on my case; I felt I had plenty of problems without that. But there she was, lacing into me, telling me that she was disappointed with me and asking if there was something going on at home that might be causing my problems in school. As much as I trusted her to be fair as she always had been, well almost always, I felt that I couldn't tell her about what had happened in my family. How embarrassing, I thought. If people knew that my dad didn't live at home and that he had left my mom because of me, there would be no living it down at school. Unsuccessful in her attempt at gaining information from me, Miss Richards sent a note home to my folks asking them to schedule a conference with her.

Things went from bad to worse. I thought how angry my parents would be and that they had enough to worry about without me creating more problems. When I left school, I saw Marty waiting for me. With a big gloating grin he asked, "Boy, it sure looks like you've gotten yourself into it again, Jamie. What did Miss Richards want with you? Do you need to write one of those dumb assignments again?"

Even if I wanted to share with him what had happened, his questions came so fast that there was hardly time to get a word in edgewise.

"No, Marty, it's not that at all." I wasn't sure that he even heard me, because he went on and on without stopping to take a breath, or to even understand what I was feeling.

"I know; she thinks it was you who marked up the chalkboard with those four letter words. Isn't that right?"

"No, Marty, you're not right; why don't we just drop it."

"Well, that's cool with me, but you're the one who's always talking about how people should be more honest with one another, and then we would all be closer in this world. Are you trying to tell me that those were all just a bunch of words you were throwing at me, huh, Jamie, huh?"

There was no denying it, that sure was what I said. But maybe it didn't work all the time. I tried to justify what I had said, but I still felt that maybe he was right. After all, he had been sorta nice to me lately.

"You're right Marty, I haven't been as straight with you as I should be."

"Well, that's more like it. So what did she really want with you, Jamie?"

"She wanted to talk to me about my grades slipping and how I need to get my folks to come in for a conference."

"Boy, that's bad news, Jamie, but I wouldn't worry too much about it; my grades stink, too."

"It's more than just bad grades; my dad doesn't live with us anymore. There's so much going on at home and I don't want to create more."

"That's a bad scene all right, but you're not the only one who's got those kind of problems. I've had three different stepfathers in the last six years; how's that for a record?"

"Gosh, Marty, I didn't know...I mean three stepfathers ...in six years, wow!"

"Yeah, ain't that something? I'm not sure if that will get me into the *Guinness Book of World Records*, but it's certainly enough, if you know what I mean."

I heard sadness in Marty's voice and I felt sorry for him and what he must have gone through during all those family changes. It was hard for me to imagine living with so many different fathers. I became concerned for myself again. I wondered if Mom would be bringing home a new father for me. Thinking of that as a possibility made me feel worse, and I decided to check it out with her when I got home. But after some more thought, I figured maybe I wouldn't. We'd have enough to talk about when she heard that Miss Richards wanted to see her.

I couldn't think of anything to say to Marty other than, "Wow! You've sure had a lot of fathers."

We walked home together and Marty talked about himself and his family life. In many ways he was like Clarence and me. He wasn't as much on top of everything as he had led us to believe. It shocked me to find out that he wasn't so different from us. I had always thought he was so tough, but that wasn't the real Marty. I wondered how he kept track of who he was, when he was so busy fooling everyone else.

My thoughts about him became confused, so I decided to drop them. I waved goodbye as he went into his house and I went on home. He certainly had given me a lot to think about, except that at that point I didn't need any more; I had enough of my own stuff to worry about.

Mom's first words to me when I got home were, "Why are you late, Jamie? You know I worry when you don't come right home from school."

I thought to myself that there was no point hiding what happened at school now. I might as well level with her and be done with it. I was quite sure it would mean off to bed with no dinner again. Oh well, what was I to do? I leveled with her. "Mom, I did come straight home from school. It's just that I had to stay there for a while."

"What did you do Jamie? Why were you kept after school?"

"This will explain it, I think," I cautiously replied.

I handed her my report card and the note from Miss Richards, and waited for the whole world to cave in on me.

"Do you have any idea why your grades have been falling?"

It was one of those questions that parents sometimes ask, even though they know the answer. She was like, testing me to see if I understood what was happening. As usual when I answered quickly, I ended up putting my foot in my mouth. I just sort of blurted out, "I don't know." Why did I say that? Whenever I did my amnesia number with an "I don't know," and Mom or Dad felt I did or should have known, it was like waving a red flag in front of a bull, or a couple of bulls.

She reacted as I expected, "Jamie, how can you tell me that you don't know what's causing your grades to go down, after bringing home this kind of report card? You're the one who's in class, not me."

Besides feeling upset since receiving that "dumb" report card, I became angry as well. Yes, I knew why my grades were sinking fast. After all, my whole life was falling apart, and I was supposed to be worried about school. All of my thoughts were there; it was the words that I was having trouble with. I might have said all of those things to Mom, but I didn't. Instead I said, "What I meant to say was that I tried my best, but everything at school kept getting harder." I wondered if she would accept that explanation. I watched closely for her reaction. But Mom didn't react, she was too busy reading the note from Miss Richards.

"Jamie, I see that your teacher wants your dad and me to come in for a conference. Did you tell her about us, I mean that we're not together?"

"No, Mom, I didn't. I felt—"

"I understand. I certainly know how you feel. This whole thing is so new and upsetting to us all."

Mom sounded much more understanding than before. I guess she needed to get past the initial shock. Well, I had survived another situation, at least for the moment. I sighed deeply and went to my room to be alone, where maybe I could sort out what I had been through that day.

CHAPTER 7

⌒

ANOTHER SIDE TO DAD

Do Parents Love Their Kids?

When Mom and Dad came to school for their meeting with Miss Richards, I waited nervously through all my classes for the news of the outcome. When I came home from school, I saw Dad's car parked in front of the house. Whatever happened at the meeting must have been so important that both he and Mom needed to talk to me about it. In a way it was like old times, with both of them together, even if they were going to lecture me.

It didn't go at all as I expected. They didn't start out being angry at me. Instead, Dad reached out and hugged me. When he held me, I could smell his after shave lotion, which I had liked from the time I was a little kid. With one of his big hands he took hold of the back of my head and held me close. At that moment I felt secure and safe. Something happened to us all; I didn't know what it was, except that it felt good. I decided not to question what was going on, but to just enjoy it. It seemed natural to close my eyes as I felt my father's warmth.

I knew that that's what love was all about, and more importantly that Dad loved me. The questions I had asked myself, about how he felt about me, were gone in that moment of warmth and sharing. My eyes filled with tears, only they weren't tears of sadness this time. When I opened my eyes, I saw Mom sitting on the couch, wiping away her tears. Tough old Dad, who hardly ever showed his emotions, was crying too. We knew that no matter what followed, that experience was never to be forgotten. We sat together quietly, allowing our eyes to speak for us. Our smiles showed the joy that we felt, following the deep connection that was made.

Dad added his comments to what Mom had said earlier, that they understood how I was affected by the changes that were taking place in our family. He also told me that Miss Richards recommended that I see a counselor, someone I could speak to about what was going on with me. He added that he felt it was a good idea for me to talk with someone about those things that were bothering me. I was surprised to hear Dad say that, considering what he had said about not believing in shrinks.

"I don't understand, Dad. Didn't you used to say that they're all a little nuts?" I asked. "You said you'd never go to a stranger and tell him what was going on in your personal life," I continued.

Dad responded, "That's true, Jamie, I can't deny it, I did say that. But you need to understand that parents' attitudes can change. When I called them shrinks and said I would never go to one of them, it was because I was afraid of looking more deeply into myself."

"I still don't understand, Dad."

Mom, seeing my confusion, joined in, "Jamie, have you ever felt there were things going on with you that made you uncomfortable? Things that you wanted to share with someone but were too frightened to talk about?"

"Yeah, I guess I have." I knew I had experienced those feelings often.

"Well, that goes on with parents as well," Mom said, "that's part of what your dad has been trying to say, about it being fearful to reveal himself to someone else."

"Most people are frightened of change, almost any change," Dad added.

"Can you remember how you felt when you transferred from elementary school where you felt comfortable, to junior high? Now, that was a big change, wasn't it?" Dad made things clear to me with his examples.

"It sure was," I responded without hesitation.

Dad continued, "Well, that's like what I was going through, Jamie. I was frightened about changes that were happening to me. But I'm not afraid now as I was then. I've learned that if I don't take risks and make changes, I'm not going to move ahead in my life. I haven't told you this before, but since Mom and I separated, we've been going to a therapist, who I also see on my own. It's not like miracles are happening for us, but it's a lot easier now than it was. Jamie, I was frightened about opening up to a stranger and I was afraid to look more deeply into myself because I didn't know what I'd find. It was easier for me to point the finger at someone else and use them as my excuse for not dealing with my fear. Now, getting back to you. . . ."

For a period of time my thoughts blanked out as Dad

continued to speak. I found it hard to keep up with him as I tried to understand everything he said. My thoughts drifted to Marty. He must also have had lots of fears and no one he felt he could talk to. His sharing with me must have been hard for him. I felt good that Marty had trusted me. I also thought about Clarence. When he almost ended his life there was no one he felt he could talk to about his problems. I couldn't believe how much there was to understand.

Dad was still explaining, when I realized I had missed some of what he had said. That bothered me, so I quickly started listening again as he continued, " . . . the important thing for you is to realize and want it for yourself. I wouldn't want you to feel that you had to go into counseling because we were pushing you. Even though I think, as your mother does, that it would be valuable to you, especially with what you've been going through."

Dad and Mom were quite persuasive when they put their minds to it. With their suggestion, and with Clarence saying how well he and his family were doing seeing a counselor, I agreed to give this counseling thing a try.

Loaded with concerns, I prepared myself for entering into something completely new to me. Thinking what it was going to be like was both scary and exciting.

One day, as I stared at the big oak tree, I noticed that its leaves were gone; it was as if they had disappeared overnight. I continued to watch it closely, not knowing exactly what else I might see, when a cold breeze blew through the window. It chilled me through and through, leaving goose bumps all over my body. Quickly closing the window, I realized another season had passed and winter was here.

Part Four

∾

WINTERTIME

The Cold of the Season
and Warmth of the Heart

CHAPTER 8

~

SHARING SECRET FEELINGS AND THOUGHTS

The Counseling Experience

Sometimes it was difficult for me to understand what was going on with Mom and Dad. Everyone else seemed to be adjusting to their situation, but I wasn't sure that they were. They continued to live in their own separate places and yet there was a lot of connection between them. Occasionally I heard Dad coming into the house after I had gone to bed. He and Mom would talk until late. Even though it was well past my bedtime, I couldn't sleep knowing that Dad was downstairs. It was exciting and confusing when I thought they might get back together, yet it didn't happen. It was also difficult to understand why Dad didn't spend time with me when he came over. Oh well, I thought, parents can be hard to understand sometimes.

I woke up earlier than usual on the day of my first appointment with the counselor. I was feeling nervous about meeting this person who everyone said was going to help me. When I arrived at his office I felt even more nervous than before. Even though it was the start of winter and already cold, I was perspiring like I do in summer. My hands were moist and cold and I kept trying to dry them on my jeans. I wished that I had taken Mom and Dad up on their offer to come in with me. Their reassurance would have helped me now. But for some unknown reason, I felt that this was something that I wanted to do on my own.

Thoughts of not going through with it went through my mind, as I slowly opened the door. A woman greeted me and I knew there would be no backing out. She seemed friendly and kind, as if she knew how nervous I was. After telling her my name, she asked me to have a seat and told me that the doctor would see me shortly. I picked up a magazine, not knowing what I had selected, and looked at the words and pictures, hoping to get my mind off how I felt. Instead, I found myself staring at it, without knowing what I was seeing.

I was interrupted from my reading when the counselor came out of his office. As he shook my hand, I thought he would notice how sweaty and nervous I was. To my surprise he didn't react at all to my clammy wet hands. Instead, he put his arm around my shoulder and as he guided me into his office he asked if I was interested in football and which team I was rooting for.

His office was kind of neat, more like a comfortable den in someone's house than a doctor's office, except for all of the certificates on the wall. He even had overstuffed chairs and a couch that looked like what we had given to the Salvation Army when we got our new furniture. On one wall was the biggest collection of books I'd ever seen. I thought of Mom when I saw his books, since she often got angry at me when the books on my shelf were messy. His were all that way; books stacked in every possible direction imaginable.

He distracted my attention from this most interesting room, almost startling me with his question. "Well now, Mr. English, how about you and I getting acquainted?" We chatted about many different things, none of which seemed too important. However, I guess it helped, because I began to feel more comfortable. The doctor must have liked asking questions, for he did a lot of that.

While we talked I couldn't help staring at him. His name was Dr. Gerald Balding, which struck me funny considering that his appearance and his name contradicted one another. For a man named Balding, he had the most hair I'd ever seen on anyone's head. He looked like he had more hair than his head could hold. I wondered if he were wearing a wig. I realized it was his own hair, and as if that wasn't enough, he also had a full beard to go with it. I wondered why his mother or wife didn't tell him how he looked and suggest that he do something about it. Maybe there was nothing that could be done about it.

Once again I was distracted by him. This time he suggested that if I would agree to call him Jerry, instead of Dr. Balding, he would call me Jamie. So that's the way it was. From the beginning of our relationship it became Jerry and Jamie, which helped keep me from cracking up about Dr. Balding being so hairy.

During our first hour together, my sweating had stopped and I was feeling much more comfortable. I left feeling glad that I had listened to Mom and Dad's advice about coming to

see Dr. Balding, I mean Jerry. Actually, I looked forward to our next appointment so that we could talk again.

In our sessions that followed, I told him about Dad's late night visits to the house and of my confusion about them. I also told him of my difficulty in just rapping with people. It was clear to me that he knew from the start it was Dad I wanted to be able to talk to. There was nothing special I needed for Dad and I to talk about. I wanted us to share what I imagined dads and sons usually talked about. Deep inside I also wanted us to be close, like I imagined he and George were.

I learned a lot from Jerry about how people communicate and how sometimes it all gets messed up. For one thing, I learned that communicating didn't only mean the speaking part, but it also included being a good listener. As he put it, "It's important if communication between two people is to be meaningful, that each one must hear what the other is saying." I thought it funny in a way, since I never had considered listening as being part of two people talking. I guess I took it for granted that people just talked to one another, and yet it made sense, since if no one is listening then talking would be a waste of time.

The more I got to know Jerry, the more I found him to be a regular guy. That made it easy for me to get past my concerns of what he was going to be like and what he would expect of me. With that out of the way, I found myself liking him. I felt more comfortable with Jerry than I had ever been with someone new. I think maybe his being relaxed helped me to relax, too.

Jerry made it clear that our relationship together was of prime importance in the work that I was to do. At first I wasn't sure what he meant, but it soon became clear. As we became closer I trusted him enough to share what was going on inside me. I even found myself enjoying it. Clarence and I were close friends, and I shared quite a bit with him. Yet there were certain things that I couldn't tell even him, which I was able to talk to Jerry about.

I told Jerry how badly I felt about myself and also how I had caused my parents to argue, which resulted in Dad moving out. His reaction at first surprised me, as it was quite different from what I was used to. Mom and Dad would have stopped me right in the middle of what I was saying to offer all kinds of reasons for me not to feel the way I did. I tried my best to listen to their advice, but my feelings didn't go away or change. The first time I told Jerry how bad I felt about what I had done, I sat there waiting for him to also tell me that I was wrong, which he didn't do. Instead, after what felt like an endless pause, he asked me what I was waiting for and suggested that I continue. Getting such an unexpected reaction, I asked him, "Do you mean to say, Jerry, that you agree with me, that I did cause Dad to leave?"

He responded quickly, "That's not what I said, Jamie. What I believe I said is that I would like to hear more of what led to your feelings that you caused your parents to take the action they did."

For the first time I felt I had permission from an adult to not only have the feelings that were mine, but to be heard, too. The dam opened that day and my feelings poured out like a rush of water through a barrier that had been gently set aside. I can't remember everything he or I said, but I can remember he encouraged me to continue and his questions helped me better understand my own thoughts. At one point

I began to cry; I thought I would never stop. Still, I could hear Jerry very quietly repeating to me, "It's OK, Jamie; it's OK to feel and it's OK to cry."

I put my arms around him as best I could, for he was such a large man. He also held me. His hug was warm and genuine and for a moment I thought I was being held by a big Teddy bear, one that was gentle, yet strong and secure. I felt safe. In my fears the streets and my school seemed like a jungle, and most of the kids I came in contact with were like animals, always ready to attack me. At that moment though, I was safe and protected by my own friendly and hairy bear. I felt freer from the dangers of those wild animals than I had in a long time. I dried my tears and sat back in my chair. We smiled, showing without words how much we cared about each other.

Through those sessions with Jerry we talked about everything that came to my mind. I'm sure that one of the things that made it so easy for me, was that he accepted me as I was. I soon realized there was more than one way to look at every issue, including how I saw myself. My negative feelings didn't disappear with one of our winter's winds, but as Jerry put it, "Neither did you become the Jamie you are that quickly." There were times that I felt sadder after we talked. Following such a session Jerry remarked, "Jamie, you're doing very well. You may not fully understand what I'm about to say, but in time it will become clearer to you. As human beings we are constantly changing and growing—"

"You mean like when I transferred from elementary school to junior high and went through all of those changes?" I repeated Dad's example, because I wanted to show him I understood.

"Yes, that's a good example, Jamie. Some of the things you went through were extremely painful at the time. Yet there was also a lot of learning for you, and learning and change do not come easily. That's what I mean when I talk about growing as a person. It's like accumulating each piece of learning that comes from your experiences, some of which are painful, and using them in a positive way to bring about good changes. Often, Jamie, as a result of how we handle those painful experiences, we either move forward and become stronger or we just continue to live with the pain."

"Will the pain I felt today help me be stronger tomorrow if I've learned from it?" I asked.

"You bet it will, Jamie. That's exactly what I mean. It all adds to our experiences and helps us in our tomorrows. I don't mean that we run around purposely looking for pain, but we don't need to run from it either when it can help us become stronger."

"I think it's clearer to me now, Jerry. I remember how much Clarence and I learned from his painful experience with those pills. Also the continuing pain I've been feeling blaming myself for Mom and Dad's problems." All of a sudden I shouted out, "I wasn't to blame; it wasn't my fault. I couldn't have made them do it and I couldn't have stopped them either, just as I couldn't have stopped Clarence from doing what he did. Jerry, I do understand. I do understand it now."

Jerry didn't respond, he just shook his head in agreement and smiled his familiar smile of approval.

Those had been painful days for me, but also different from what I had gone through before. At least now I was able to see some light at the end of the tunnel, where in the past there had been nothing but darkness and confusion.

Later as I sat in the quiet of my room, I thought about what had taken place with Jerry, and I felt proud of myself. It was as if I had accomplished something major, and the truth was I had. I clearly remembered saying to Jerry I wasn't to blame for what happened to Mom and Dad. Golly, I thought, can it be true? And yet I knew it was. It felt like I had removed a heavy weight from around my neck that I had been carrying for a long time and I was happy to see it go.

There were some tough times for me during that period as I continued to learn more about myself. With new learning, I began to like the person I was. There's no doubt in my mind, as I look back at what I went through, that it was all worth it, for I was able to feel myself changing and growing, and it was exciting.

CHAPTER 9

⌒

COMING TOGETHER AS EQUALS

Needing to Be Who You Are

Winter had always been a special time for me, with Thanksgiving and Christmas and our family get togethers. That year I looked forward to the holidays as always, except that there was something going on that made it feel different. I had questions going around in my head that wouldn't quit, like was Dad going to be with us for Thanksgiving and was George coming home for the holidays?

The real issue and the major question was: What would Thanksgiving be like for us, and how different would it be with Mom and Dad living separately? It didn't take long for some of my questions to be answered. Mom told me that George would be home for Thanksgiving, and that he and I would have a double celebration that year. We would have dinner at home with Mom, and dessert with Dad and his new lady friend. I was shocked to hear that Dad had a girl friend.

But, it didn't affect me for too long, as I found myself caught up in the news that my brother George was coming home in a few days. The excitement built for me as I thought of George and me being together again. The more I thought about what it was going to be like to have him at home, the harder it was to wait for those days to pass.

On the day he arrived I woke up early and listened quietly for some sounds of life in the house. The sun hadn't come up yet and everything was quiet. Lying in bed I remembered the fun George and I used to have together. I waited anxiously for the day to start. Then I heard Mom in the kitchen, so I jumped excitedly out of bed almost flying down the stairs. Mom was also excited. She smiled at me, and then asked, "Jamie, do you know today's the day George is coming home?"

No kidding, I said to myself. Why else would I have been up since dawn? Oh well, we kids need to have patience with our parents, so I replied respectfully, "I sure do, Mom. By the way, what's for breakfast?"

"There are times I think food is the only thing you have on your mind," she said.

She didn't realize that I was trying to use what little sense of humor I had, when really I couldn't have cared less about breakfast. The only thing on my mind was that George would be home in a few hours.

Those hours moved slowly, as I kept watching for Dad's car. Finally he arrived and we all left for the airport. Everyone was excited as George's plane taxied to the terminal. It was the biggest jet I'd ever seen. I wondered how the combined weight of all those people and their baggage could remain in the air powered only by its jet engines.

101

Dad reached over and took my hand. I was afraid to look down at our hands for fear that what I felt wasn't really happening, and that my mind was playing tricks on me. But it was real, for I felt him gently squeeze my hand as he looked at me and smiled. He was excited, as we all were, that George would soon be with us, but there was much more to his smile. I saw something glowing in Dad that I hadn't seen for a long time.

My mind shifted from George and his arrival, to how good it was to see Dad so happy. Seeing him that way reminded me of when I was much younger and Mom and Dad would take George and me to the movies for our family night out. During the movie, when something funny happened and Mom and Dad laughed, I'd laugh, too, as I shared their enjoyment. This was that kind of an experience for me.

Suddenly Dad released my hand and quickly moved forward to greet George. There he was. My heart beat faster as I saw Mom and Dad throw their arms around him. When they let go, George and I stared at each other for a second and then we grabbed each other. While we hugged, I felt him saying things to me, even though a word hadn't been spoken. As far back as I could remember, we'd always had that ability to feel what was going on with each other.

The ride home from the airport was slower than usual, due to the recent snows, and the ice just beneath its surface. Dad was quiet as he often was when he concentrated on his driving. The rest of us made up for his silence with our nonstop chatter. There was much catching up to do. George asked questions continuously as he tried to get caught up on all of the latest happenings. His questions stayed clear of one sensitive area, the status of Mom and Dad.

While carrying George's bags into the house, I noticed how he looked at the house and the neighborhood. He took it all in, digesting the familiar scenes like a hungry person enjoying a hearty meal. George had a lot of old memories to renew, while I only thought about my older brother being home again.

We sat in the living room, enjoying the fire in the fireplace and also the warmth from our family bond. None of us wanted to think about what we knew would soon take place: Dad's return to his own apartment. But for that moment the whole family was together. It became even more like the old days when Mom brought out the hot chocolate. George's eyes sparkled as he saw the large cups with melted marshmellows floating on top. That was one of Mom's specialties for taking the chill out of a winter night, and none of us had forgotten it. That night we talked and drank hot chocolate as if there was no tomorrow. I felt good about not needing to go to bed early on that special occasion. Instead I stayed up with the others until we all decided we had best call it a day. As Dad left, he hugged each of us, including Mom. It was a heavy scene for George, who until then hadn't seen Dad leave the house where we had lived together for so many years. George couldn't control his emotions; he became teary eyed, and we felt that moment with him.

The following day Mom made George his favorite breakfast of orange juice; pancakes, as he claimed only Mom could make them with strawberry syrup; sausages, burnt beyond recognition; and a mug of milk. George developed a habit at an early age of drinking his milk in a coffee mug, so he would feel like he was drinking coffee like Mom and Dad. Funny thing is, as he got older, he never did acquire a taste for coffee. To this day he still enjoys his milk in a mug. I wondered what good old Dr. Balding would have said about that.

After breakfast George and I dressed warmly at Mom's insistence and went for a walk. George claimed he wanted to see how the neighborhood had changed. But I knew he wanted, as I did, for us to spend some time alone. It was one of those things that had been missing for me since George left for school. We walked for a long time, each of us chatting about nothing in particular; it was our own brand of small talk.

I went on and on about about my friends, Clarence, Diane, and Marty, and of my experiences in junior high. He told me about college life and his friends, including his special friend Linda. He asked me not to say anything about her until he told Mom and Dad. But it was pretty much of a certainty that they would become engaged in the near future. I was excited for George and his happiness, yet it also bothered me that I might be losing him. George went on and on about how great California and Los Angeles were. When he told me about kids swimming in the wintertime, and about many of the homes having swimming pools, it was hard for me to picture. "Wow! I couldn't imagine us having a swimming pool in our back yard," I told him.

During our walk to the rocky area down by the brook, he told me of a place he liked near the ocean in California, which reminded him of where we were. He promised he would take me there when I came out on a visit. We carefully selected two flat rocks next to each other, brushed off the snow, and made ourselves at home. I tried to ignore the dampness I felt on my rear, and instead thought of how great it was being there with George. I told him that before he returned to school I wanted to share my favorite spot with him, even though that patch of grass wouldn't be too appealing at that time of year. He made it clear he'd be happy to see any place that was important to me.

After covering most of our subjects of interest, George got to the one that hadn't been touched at all. He was careful when he started talking about the situation of Mom, Dad, and me. At the same time he wanted to know everything that had happened. I had no problem sharing our family stuff with him. I felt it had been mine alone for too long. I told him at first I blamed myself, but then I felt it hadn't been my fault. George told me that he too felt guilty, but not in the same way. His guilt had to do with being so far away when all of this was going on and not being able to be with me when I needed him.

I told him of my therapy with Jerry and how it had helped me through much of the rough times. I also shared my belief that I had become a stronger person as a result of my counseling. I went into some of the details of what happened in therapy, which I had not told anyone else. George showed a lot of interest in what I had done. He indicated he was quite interested in psychology and had even switched his major from engineering to clinical psychology. Some day, he said, he would like helping people on a personal basis, instead of spending his life over a drawing board.

He expressed how concerned he had been about the way I used to put myself down, and how badly he felt when Dad was less than flattering in his comments about me. My reaction was quick, "George, that's the understatement of the year. I love Dad with all of my heart, but it was terrible for me constantly being compared to you, who could do no wrong."

"Gosh! I didn't know. I mean—"

"Please, George, there's no need for you to apologize, it wasn't your fault. As a matter of fact, a good part of it was due to my own problem. I just wasn't strong enough to take what was being said without it leaving me feeling hurt."

"Jamie, I never fully realized what you were going through."

"I don't think you could have done anything about it, George, even if you knew."

"Well, I certainly could have been more supportive to you," he said.

"One of the things I've learned is that no one can help me but me. I don't mean to take away from what I've learned from Jerry. Without him I'd still be where I was, not liking myself and blaming others for how I am. You know, in a way, Dad also deserves some credit."

"Dad?" George asked.

"Yes, Dad. If it weren't for him, I wouldn't have gone into therapy. He's quite the salesman, you know. Dad's learned a lot about himself, too, and I think that he's changing for the better. The unfortunate part is that it's taken what he and Mom have been going through to bring it about. I can't believe what I'm about to say, but I'll say it anyway. If their marriage needs to end for them to become better and stronger, then I think . . . maybe it's all worthwhile."

"Jamie, I don't know that I'd go that far, but I can tell you this, you've sure grown up since I last saw you. And the way you're going, you won't ever need to worry about having been compared to me. If anything, I'm sure that I could learn a lot from you."

107

"Thanks, George. It really means a lot hearing you say that. The most important thing I've learned from my therapy, which I needed to understand, is that I could never be another George. As much as I love and admire you, I need to be me."

"Well, my brother, I do believe I've gained more from you on our little walk than I did all last semester at the University. The best thing I've learned is that now I can get on with my life with Linda knowing that you're going to be OK."

We shook hands, and as we looked at each other, our smiles grew into laughter. That was a special time for us. It was a time of coming together as brothers and as equals. I sighed deeply as I thought how important he was to me, and of how much I loved him.

CHAPTER 10

～

TWO THANKSGIVING DINNERS

When Parents Live Apart

Waking up on a cold winter morning can be a treat, especially when it's a holiday. It meant no school and no need for getting up early. As I woke up that morning, knowing it was a holiday, I remained snuggled up under my heavy comforter, keeping nice and warm. I raised my head just enough to see out the window. The view was great; another snow had fallen while I slept. The snow had left a beautiful white blanket on the ground. Yet, seeing it chilled me, so I put my head under the covers with my eyes and nose barely showing. I stayed that way, enjoying the warmth of my bed, until the smell of Mom's cooking found its way into my bedroom. Knowing that this was no ordinary breakfast I smelled, it became too much for me and my appetite to take. Suddenly it struck me that this was Thanksgiving Day, and Mom always started cooking early on holidays.

I wasn't the first one to have my taste buds awakened; George beat me to it. He was already busily eating breakfast when I came downstairs. He announced my arrival like old times, "Well, look who's decided to wake up. If it isn't Prince Jamie himself. We thought you would be sleeping the day away, Your Highness. After all, who has time for such things as breakfast with pancakes, sausages, and the like, especially with a busy schedule like yours, sire."

"I can't believe it. Are we having pancakes again?" My response was also typical of our old family days together. "Mom, I know that you have one son, who shall go nameless for the moment, who's a pancake freak, but does that mean we all must join his cult?"

"You boys stop it now. You're no sooner together for a day, than things are back to normal, whatever that is. Jamie, you know how George is about pancakes, so just relax. You can have whatever you like for breakfast, too."

"That's great, Mom. How about some of your famous strawberry shortcake and two large scoops of vanilla ice cream, covered with—"

"That will be enough from you young man. Just sit down and I'll get you some bacon and eggs."

Mom returned to the job she liked best, cooking for her family. George and I smiled at each other as he affectionately reached out and grabbed my arm. Fooling around at breakfast was one way we showed that we cared. At other times, I was less nervy and more sensitive to what was said. But, I know that with George around I acted differently; it was safer and easier for me to follow his lead.

Mom continued her Thanksgiving preparations while George and I watched a football game on television. I never

was much of a sports fan, but it was fun watching with George. I even cheered and got caught up in the excitement just as he did. At one point I paused long enough to think how good it felt having a brother around to share things with.

When I heard that Aunt Ethel and Uncle Frank were joining us for our holiday dinner, it relieved some of my concerns about leaving Mom alone on Thanksgiving. I had been a little panicky about how things would be for her when we left for Dad's.

Dinner was great as always. There's no two ways about it, Mom was a fantastic cook. The poor old turkey looked like it had been attacked by hungry vultures. Afterwards, Uncle Frank amused us with his tales of days gone by when he was in show business. It was an ongoing ritual that everyone expected and went along with. Uncle Frank told us his fantastic stories and we were his audience. I suspected that he got to believing the things he told us, and after a while it was hard to know what did take place and what was just his imagination. We all found his stories entertaining, so it didn't matter one way or another. I liked hearing of his adventures, and if he changed them a little to make them more interesting, then he did what he set out to do, and that didn't bother me at all.

George stared at me and then at his watch; I knew it was time for us to leave. It felt strange going from one dinner to another. It wasn't as if we minded, for we looked forward to spending time with Dad. But it was unusual, and took a little getting used to.

George drove cautiously. He explained, "In California we don't have snow and ice to deal with, just rain, oil, and earthquakes."

I must be growing up, I thought, because I didn't reply with my usual "Really, George." Besides, I knew that joking was his way of relieving tension.

When we arrived, Dad was glad to see us and greeted us warmly. We were introduced to two of his friends from work and their wives, who had been there for dinner. Dad asked if we were still hungry and could handle some more turkey. George and I looked at each other wondering if we were expected to have a second meal with Dad and if we should do it even though we were full. After all, we didn't want to hurt his feelings. Dad understood what was going on with us and quickly followed up with, "If you've had enough turkey, you might want to leave some room for our great dessert. How about that, boys?"

Dad saved the day. Full as we might be, we never were too full when it came to dessert. So we quickly nodded in agreement to his offer. After we sat down with his friends, a woman came out of the kitchen carrying a cake. I wondered for an instant where her husband was. Then Dad introduced us and I realized she was Dad's friend. Her name was Marian, and she seemed nice enough and friendly, but I wasn't buying it. It was easy to tell that George liked her, but I didn't care. I wasn't about to be friendly, because I felt it wouldn't be fair to Mom. George's lack of loyalty puzzled me; how could he act so friendly to that woman?

I was sure Marian was able to sense my feelings. She continued being friendly the rest of the evening, but she knew what was going on with me. In spite of that, she didn't try to do or say anything to change how I felt. Dad also knew I was in a strange mood.

At one point, he asked George and me to join him in the bedroom, where he attempted to explain that it was a natural thing for both Mom and him to have friends. He told us that Marian had been helpful to him when he needed a friend and that he hoped we would accept her. He stressed that it was important to him that we all get along. George assured Dad that he understood and that the important thing was that Mom and he be happy. I didn't say much; I was too caught up in feeling sorry for Mom and I guess for myself. To me it meant that my dream of us all being together again was not going to happen.

On our way home George and I talked about Mom, Dad,

and Marian. We also discussed our feelings and reactions to what was going on. I tried hard to hear what George was explaining and to understand Dad's side of it. But, in spite of everything, I couldn't accept some strange woman taking Dad away from Mom. It was also difficult for me to accept that Dad seemed so happy with Marian and wanted to be with her.

CHAPTER 11

∼

BREAKING OUT OF THE FEAR CYCLE

Learning to Face Life

It wasn't until I started seeing Jerry again, following our double Thanksgiving, that things became clearer to me. My way of dealing with the latest happenings in my life, namely Dad and Marian, hadn't been working too well for me or for anyone else. I was caught up in needing to remake our family life as it used to be. When that didn't happen, my emotions once again went haywire. I needed to backtrack a little, looking inside myself again to see what I might do to get over how I was feeling.

For one thing, I knew I felt hurt and rejected when I met Marian. My experience at Thanksgiving added to the fear I already had: that Mom and Dad might never come back together. My thoughts began to come true when Marian appeared. Remembering all the work and time that went into getting rid of my guilt about Mom and Dad's separation,

I didn't want to mess up all that had been gained with what I was then experiencing. I realized that more work needed to be done and I thought I'd better begin. This time, I returned to Jerry without feeling nervous or having clammy hands.

Jerry hadn't changed since I last saw him, not that I had expected any major changes. His books were still messy as ever, but this time I saw them differently than before. My thought was that each and every book was important to him. They didn't just decorate his bookcase; he used them. Jerry and I talked about my concerns regarding Mom and Dad not getting back together again. He responded that he understood my concern. He said that I was trying to predict an outcome that was beyond his or my control. He went on to point out that there was something within my control that I could do something about, if I chose to. I told him I was willing to do anything that would help. "Good," he said, "then suppose we start with your fears."

"My fears? What do you mean?"

"Jamie, it's your fears that are blocking you concerning your parents. And you're going to need to get past them, before you can comfortably get on with the rest of your life." He patiently explained, "The possibility is real that your parents may not come back together; your ability to face it, Jamie, is what we need to work on." His look was much more serious than he had shown before.

I wanted him to assure me that Mom and Dad would get back together, which wasn't happening, so I shouted in anger that I couldn't, nor did I want to face it. He remained quiet, listening carefully to me, as I voiced my feelings. Then once again he spoke about fear and what happens when people are unwilling to face it. He explained how easy it was to get caught up in what he referred to as a "fear cycle." "It's important that you understand how it works, and how people get locked into this cycle," he explained. "When we become frightened of something, we have choices regarding how we can handle it. Often we choose what we think will be the least painful way out, which is to remove ourselves from needing to deal with the situation we fear. Are you following me so far?" he asked.

"Yes, I think so," I replied.

"It will become clearer to you as we go on," he assured me. "As an example, Jamie, if you become frightened, and it doesn't matter of whom or what, and then you try to dodge it, temporarily you might be relieved by not facing it. But it's important for you to remember that if you haven't dealt with the fear it stays with you. Most fears don't go away by themselves. As a matter of fact, very often the opposite occurs; they get bigger and stronger, feeding on one another as they grow."

I liked the way Jerry explained things, and often I could see pictures in my mind of what he described. In this case, I saw ugly little creatures with "fear" printed on their T-shirts, who kept growing larger and larger until they finally burst right out of their shirts.

Jerry continued, "Those fears that we run from stay in what I call a fear cycle, which is like a big circle that goes around and around, and which we are unable to break out of."

Again I saw those fat little fear characters with their torn T-shirts, only this time they were all riding on a merry-go-round, one that was going very fast.

"So we stay in that circle, suffering, because we're locked

in to our fears that don't go away. Soon we find that we're unable to enjoy the nice things and the nice people around us, because we're caught up in our fears. As you can see, Jamie, it does become a self-limiting situation."

I understood what Jerry meant. It was exactly how I handled situations and people in my life, and I told him so. "Jerry, that's exactly what I've been doing. I've been running and hiding from people and things that frighten me. It's gotten so bad that the only time I feel free of it all is when I'm alone."

Jerry responded, "Do those things that bother you go away when you isolate yourself?"

"Only for a while, when I hide in my room or in my secret place. But when I come out again, they're still there. It's as if they wait for me to come out." I felt myself getting upset as I described how I had lived my life.

"What's going on with you right now, Jamie?" he asked as he recognized what I was going through.

"I'm feeling those feelings again as I talk to you about them," I answered.

"Jamie, it's important that you understand what those feelings are. Would you be willing to say it out loud with me?" He continued, "Right now I am feeling..."

Jerry stopped in the middle of his sentence, as I continued, "...I'm feeling frightened!"

"Does it surprise you, that you're feeling frightened?" he asked.

"No...I'm fearful of so many things," I replied.

"That's OK, Jamie. The fact is that once you can admit it to yourself, then you've started fighting back. Now we can explore some positive choices for dealing with and getting

119

out of your fear cycle. First, you need to face your fear head-on and then diffuse it."

"Diffuse it?" I questioned.

"I mean, that you take the power out of your fear, and in so doing, you weaken it. Then you can return that energy which you've been giving to your fears to where it belongs, with you."

"You make it sound so easy, Jerry," I said.

"I don't want to mislead you; it's not easy. It requires lots of work, but it's certainly a lot easier than living with fears the rest of your life. It hasn't been easy for you, has it, Jamie, running away from what frightens you, especially when those things are with you all the time?"

"No, it hasn't been easy for me at all, Jerry. I don't like playing alone and being by myself and frightened all the time. I've been this way because it's the only way I've known."

As I spoke of what I had been going through, tears came to my eyes. Jerry, feeling my hurt, reached out and took hold of both my hands.

"Yes, I know, Jamie, but now you have another choice, and I'm here to help you with it. Together we will look at each of your fears and work through them, one at a time. Agreed?"

I nodded my head in acceptance.

"Then let's shake on it, partner."

I felt in his shake that he meant what he was saying, and I did, too.

"Now, in regard to your fears, what thoughts do you have on where you might start?"

I answered, feeling more sure of myself than I had in a long time, "I know exactly where I'll start. I'm going to face that fear regarding Mom and Dad head-on."

"What does that mean in terms of action? What are you going to do?" he asked.

"I'm going to call Dad and ask him if he and Marian and I, just the three of us, can go to dinner together, and then maybe we could talk and get to know each other. How does that sound, Jerry?"

"It sounds to me like you're going to face that fear head-on, and I'll bet you're going to beat it. Yes, Jamie, I feel there's no stopping you now. Like the rest of us, you may experience some setbacks from time to time, but you can tell that fear cycle to watch out, because you're breaking out."

His encouragement meant a lot to me. "I want you to know that I haven't felt this good about myself as far back as I can remember. Can you believe it, I actually feel proud of myself. Jerry, thank you for everything you've done for me," I said.

"I know you feel better about yourself, Jamie. And as much as I don't want to minimize your appreciation of my help, I believe you need to thank yourself, because you're the one who's been doing the work. I want you to know how proud I am of how well you've done. If you recall when we first met, I told you that the responsibility for any changes you made towards improving yourself were to be yours. As much as I was, and am willing to be there for you, and to help you, you needed to be willing to do the work. So I thank you for being so motivated and for working so hard."

I went home feeling very good and wanting to call Dad, so that we could arrange our get-together.

In the few days that passed there was so much that took place. To begin with, I met with Dad and Marian and it really went well. I found that once I allowed myself to be open to her, that Marian was an OK lady. It was obvious to me that she meant a lot to Dad. I could tell that he was happy with her and also with what I was doing to become a part of their lives.

George met my friends, Clarence, Diane, and Marty, and willingly put up with their endless questions about California and what it was like. They especially wanted to know if it was true that people were actually swimming while we were up to our ankles in snow. There we were, talking about people swimming, while we wore heavy jackets and ear muffs, with steam coming out of our mouths when we spoke. He assured us that it was true, and then told us more of that place so far away. My friends enjoyed George, and I was happy that he liked them, too.

Afterwards, when he and I were alone, I asked him what he thought of Diane. He answered, "Jamie, she's a knockout, and she has brains, too. Don't let her get away from you."

When I went to bed that night I kept hearing George's advice to me about Diane. Although he wasn't there to hear me, I answered him anyway, "I don't intend to let her get away."

George left that next morning, returning to California, Linda, and his studies. We were sad that once again he was leaving us. Mom, Dad, and I went to the airport to see him off. For George and me, the time that we had spent together would never be forgotten. It had been a special time for us, because we became closer than before. Although there were tears and sadness when his plane took off, I was left with good feelings about his visit and what we had created for ourselves.

As the old saying goes, "My, how time flies when you're having fun." I had fun like I never had before, and time moved quickly for me. The days and weeks flew by and I enjoyed the experience of facing the world with the excitement of the new me. I was less frightened of new situations and even got to the point where I felt challenged by them. At times, I had trouble fully accepting who I was. I found myself even asking, "Could this be the same kid who used to hide from people?" I even found myself enjoying meeting new people.

Getting so that I could deal with my fears and enjoy my new friends was much like an experience Diane had. When she first learned to ride a horse, she was frightened by how high she was above the ground when she sat on him. But, once she learned to ride she became comfortable with the height and wanted to ride all the time. So there I was, more comfortable with people and wanting to make up for my lost time. Like Diane, I, too, wasn't able to get enough of it.

Christmas came and went, as did much of the winter. We exchanged presents, but our holiday was a little empty without George. He spent the holidays that year with Linda's family. Her folks were anxious to meet this young man Linda kept writing about. I couldn't blame them, since we too wanted to meet Linda.

Mom and Dad's divorce became final. That was hard on Mom, I know, not that she had any hopes of them getting back together. She was already clear about that when she spoke to me. She said, "I'll never regret the years that your father and I were together, for many of those years were good ones. Besides, if it wasn't for us being together, we wouldn't have had you and your brother, and the joy that you have brought to us."

She showed no signs of anger toward Dad, at least not

when she was with me. Instead, she often spoke in kind terms of Marian and how she was good for him. Mom told me the thing that upset her most about getting the final divorce papers was that it marked the end of a major period in her life, and the start of another. She sounded a little concerned about the unknowns that awaited her in her new life as a single woman.

Knowing Mom as well as I did, I felt that she would get through it OK, and besides, I knew there wasn't anything I could do, except be supportive to her. As the man of the family, I promised to be as helpful as I could. She smiled at me with the most tender expression I ever saw, and then held me close. She whispered, "My big man, Jamie. You are indeed my big man; no longer are you my little boy."

I had grown, in more ways than measurement of height or years. And getting over some of my fears was not the only change that had taken place for me. I began to appreciate myself; no longer was I stuck in my negative thinking about who and what I was. I had begun to see another side that I wasn't able to see before, and with it I could more easily accept that I was OK. I would never have believed in a million years that so many good things could have taken place for me by just changing my thinking about myself, and yet they had.

CHAPTER 12

‿

A TIME FOR SAYING GOODBYE

Changes in Relationships

A few more winters passed, and with them some important events highlighted my memory of that period. For one thing, George graduated from college, and while working went on to graduate school. He and Linda were married and took up permanent residence in California, in some small beach community he called Santa Monica. Dad and Marian also were married. I'm happy to say that I became close with both of them, and that I found Marian to be the wonderful person that Dad always said she was.

During that period of those two marriages, a lot of traveling took place. George and Linda came to Dad and Marian's wedding and all of us here went to George and Linda's wedding in California. I had a great time in California, seeing all the sights I had heard so much about. It was really a dream come true for me, and best of all, I finally had a sister. Even if she was called a sister-in-law, to me she was my sister, and a neat one at that. Linda and I became instant pals and she took me everywhere.

We went on guided tours of the movie stars' homes, Hollywood Boulevard, and even the famous Hollywood and Vine, which didn't look anything like I thought it would. The most exciting part of the Hollywood tour took place at the Chinese Theatre, where I found out that Elvis Presley and I wore the same size shoes.

The newlyweds even invited me to come to California and stay with them for a whole summer. Wow, a whole summer in California; how could anybody have been so lucky. When I came home from that trip I felt great, like I was sitting on top of the world.

At that time Mom and I were still a twosome, but it looked like it wasn't going to stay that way for long. She had been seeing a guy named Fred and the two of them had been making plans for their future together. As far as my friends and I were concerned, we graduated from Farnsworth and went on to Washington High. Even after leaving junior high, I still kept my friendship with Miss Richards, who was helpful to me in overcoming many of my problems. It's doubtful that I would have gone into counseling if it hadn't been for her. That I might have remained as I had been throughout my whole life was a frightening thought.

A pleasant surprise for my family and myself, following my counseling, was that my grades in school improved. It became a lot easier to motivate myself and to concentrate on learning when I wasn't so preoccupied with negative feelings.

Clarence, on the other hand, was still not doing great. Even though the two of us spent a lot of time talking, I felt his uneasiness with me and at times some anger at my involvement with other kids. In a way I could understand how he felt, because for a long time it was just the two of us in our own little world. I knew that Clarence would always be special to me, but I also needed to experience others. In a way it was sad, but like Jerry used to say, "Not all people grow at the same rate. Even husbands and wives sometimes grow apart." Friends are no different. As I was able to relate to and feel comfortable with more kids, Clarence wasn't quite ready to expand his friendships yet.

I remembered the pledge that Clarence and I had made to each other: to be friends forever even after we marry. In spite of my changing needs I made every effort to remain friends with him. I hoped that he would continue to accept me, even if I was different from the person he first met.

Another positive result of my counseling and learning to like myself, was that I gained confidence in being with Diane. I started taking more risks, like telling her that I wanted us to always be together. Our relationship was good for a long time, but then it moved in a different direction. After our second year in high school, Diane and I were still close, but we were no longer boyfriend and girl friend. It was Diane's parents' idea; they thought it was best for her to date and experience others. We went along with it. The truth was, that with the pressure applied to her, we didn't have much choice.

My dad, the wise old philosopher tried to make me feel better by saying, "If your relationship with Diane is meant to be, it will be, in spite of everything and everybody." His words helped a little; at least there was some hope for us, but I still felt sad.

Going to the same school and seeing each other every day was difficult for us. We decided to talk about it, hoping that would help us feel better. Diane, looking as sad as I felt, started the conversation. "I'm sorry that we can't continue going steady, but I don't know what else we can do about it. You know my mother and father were very firm about what they want for me."

"Yes, I know, Diane, but that still doesn't make it OK. We care so much about each other and I want us to be married someday. Isn't that important, too?" I asked.

"Of course it's important. I argued with my parents, but I can't go against what they told me," she answered.

"I know that you've always been close to your parents and I sure don't want to cause any problems between you, but—"

"Jamie, please hear me for just a minute," she pleaded.

I interrupted as I tried to get her to understand what I felt, when in frustration she cried out, "Why can't anyone hear me?"

Her plea was very familiar to me. It was one which I'd asked myself for many years, and she was able to say it out loud. It caused me to think about what Jerry told me, "You need to listen and really hear what people say." As well as I could, I shut out my thoughts of what I wanted to say, and gave her my full attention. She continued, "I know this is hard on both of us. Still, my parents asked that we give ourselves a chance by dating others. Can't we try it their way for a while and see how things go?"

Caring as much about her as I did, I couldn't ignore what she asked. I knew she was caught in the middle between her parents and myself, and I didn't want to make things more difficult. So I told her, "OK, Diane, we'll give it a try, but I

know I'll never stop loving you."

"Thank you for being so understanding, Jamie. I love you too," she said. I held her close. Loving Diane more than ever, I truly heard what she said and wanted what would be best for her.

Diane was very popular in high school. She became a cheerleader and dated some of the football players. This added more pain to what I was already feeling, especially when I saw her with those other guys. After giving the situation a lot of thought, I decided the only way to beat the system was to join it, so I tried out for the team and made it. I figured as long as she was dating the players, I might as well be one of them. Without wanting to sound like my ego had exploded, the truth was I made the first string team and became one heck of a good quarterback. I also enjoyed becoming popular too. But, even though I dated some pretty babes, my eyes and thoughts were always on Diane.

CHAPTER 13

⌒

MARTY'S CRAZY STUNT

Peer Pressure and Drugs

During our high school years, Marty remained the same old character, even continuing his crazy stunts. It got to the point where he would do almost anything to prove himself and to be accepted by the other kids. This need of his grew stronger as we got older. There was a particular event that took place in which Marty, and his need to be one of the boys, could have gotten us all into a lot of serious trouble.

The in thing for many of the kids who were into playing the big shot role was to experiment with drugs. If there was a big shot role to be played, you can bet Marty needed to be a part of it, and he was. He not only smoked grass, but he did it in school. He claimed that the danger of being caught smoking pot in school added to the excitement. I knew that he was trying desperately to be part of the in crowd with the older kids. He would accept dares from them to do what I felt were dangerous and crazy things, just so he could feel he belonged.

Their childish prodding worked easily with Marty. I would hear them telling him that if he wanted to be a member of their club, he would have to prove he was worthy, by showing them he had courage. They would tell him what he had to do and then they would call him chicken if he didn't do it. Well, nothing worked better with Marty if you were trying to get him to do something. Call him chicken and you could guarantee he'd do it, no matter what it was.

Also typical of Marty was his need to have company when he jumped into another scheme. On that particular day who did he choose to be his companion in his mission of madness? None other than me, except that I wasn't about to buy into his craziness. I did everything I could to convince him that he shouldn't do it either. He tried calling me chicken, thinking that if it worked on him it would work on me, but it didn't. It was difficult not laughing at how obvious he was in copying the other kid's stuff. Yet I was concerned about him and what he was getting into.

In one of my quiet moments I wondered what my response would've been to this situation, if it had happened during my period of unhappiness. Would I have been dumb enough to have been involved in the drug scene, too? The answer I got wasn't clear. I didn't think I would've gotten into drugs to escape sadness and to be accepted, but the temptation would have been there. I was thankful that I got my act straightened out without needing to buy into that kind of escape. One thing I was sure about was I wouldn't have gotten into the kind of crazy risk taking that Marty had. But then his way of dealing with how he felt about himself was always different than mine.

I suspected that many of the kids in school who were into

drugs were running from things they couldn't handle. It was obvious the main thing they couldn't handle was themselves. The more I thought of it, the more I felt sorry for Marty.

I pleaded with him to reconsider, and to look carefully at the risks involved in what he was planning. He claimed he knew what he was doing, and he was going to prove to everyone that he wasn't chicken. On the day of the big dare Marty came to school ready to do his thing. I knew little of his stunt, except that it had something to do with the principal of the school. He wouldn't say much except that everyone would soon know about it and take notice of him. Clarence and I decided there was nothing we could do about it, so like everyone else, we waited.

Marty became well known that day, but in the wrong kind of way. About two hours into the school day the fire alarm went off, and we were all marched out of school. Most of us thought it was just another fire drill, except the teachers and the principal knew it wasn't planned. Clarence and I looked at each other and knew that it had to be Marty's thing. Both of us shook our heads in disbelief as we said, "Oh no, Marty, you didn't."

But sure enough, Marty did. The fire engines arrived, and when the kids saw them, the excitement was felt everywhere. Those kids who had prodded Marty into this mess stood there laughing, as they enjoyed what they had created. Clarence and I looked everywhere for Marty, but we couldn't find him. We figured he must still be in the building and that the craziness of his prank wasn't over yet. The firemen rushed into our school, dragging their hoses, as they looked for the fire. A few of them came out and spoke to our principal, and then took him back inside. Our curiosity was

134

killing us as we waited, not knowing what had happened. After a period of standing around and watching, our teachers led us back to our classes.

We were given a minimum amount of information. They told us that it had not been a fire, and to stay away from Mr. Jenkins' office. It was impossible to get any work done the rest of that day; we were too caught up with the stories going around about what had happened. We were certain that Marty was in serious trouble, for it was his name that was connected to all the rumors. Finally the news came out, and unfortunately it was true. Marty, stoned to the point of not knowing, caring, or having any fear of what he was doing, had attached a container of smoldering marijuana to one of the sprinklers above Mr. Jenkins' desk. Then, instead of removing himself from the scene, he stayed there, seated on Mr. Jenkins' desk, while the water from the sprinkler poured down on him.

Marty hadn't counted on the sprinklers automatically setting off the alarm system. He also didn't count on getting so high on pot that he wasn't able to get off Mr. Jenkins' desk. Marty became the joke of the school. I couldn't help feeling sorry for him. Poor Marty. In his need for acceptance he became an outcast, and everyone at school laughed at him. Well, maybe not everyone; Clarence, Diane, and I didn't laugh, and neither did Marty.

Talk about punishment; he got it. The school expelled Marty, and his parents restricted him from all outside activities. He was able to handle the punishment for he knew he deserved it. The hardest part was being rejected by his so-called friends. Marty had hit rock bottom. Throughout that period, and after returning to school, Diane, Clarence, and I stood by him. We were the only friends he had.

When his expulsion was over, he was offered the option of transferring to another school where he could have a fresh start. Instead, Marty asked Mr. Jenkins to give him another chance and let him return to Washington High so he could face what he needed to. We were impressed with his courage in coming back to the school where it all had happened. Under the same circumstances I don't think I could have come back as he did.

For the first time, I saw Marty differently. I respected him for his courage. As far as I knew, and by then I knew Marty well, that was the last time he experienced drugs. In the years that followed, and in the process of his growth, Marty continued learning about himself.

My life was moving along nicely. Everything was going well for Mom and her new husband Fred, and Dad and Marian also were enjoying their life together. The only problem was that Dad's health was not what it used to be. He had become quite ill, and his doctor was concerned with the difficulty he was having in regaining his strength.

He became so affected by the cold weather as the winter went on that he had to remain indoors. We all worried about him. His doctor told us that Dad was no longer able to physically handle our fierce winters with their ice and snow. He recommended that Dad move to a warmer climate. We were all shocked about their making a change of this kind. But it didn't take them long to decide that it needed to be done, and they made plans for moving.

They considered Florida and California as possible places to live, but when it came to deciding, the choice was easy. With George and his family in California, the decision was made to go west. And so it happened; they made their big move. My loss was George's gain. The pain was especially hard for me, as I had grown close to both Dad and Marian. In a special kind of way Dad had become dear to me. He and I would talk for hours, moving from subject to subject without either of us getting bored. It was great for me because nothing was off limits in our conversations. The most important change in our father-son relationship was our ability to communicate and to feel comfortable with one another. My cries of "Why can't anyone hear me?" had been answered. All the obstacles that had blocked us from becoming close during the earlier period of my life had, with time and a lot of work, resolved themselves. I not only admired and respected Dad, but also found him to be someone who I enjoyed spending time with. The one thing I wanted in my youth was to become close with him; finally having it, I was going to lose it.

With his moving, I experienced loneliness and feelings of loss. But after I had time to think about it, I set aside my feelings of self-pity. Realizing that this was not a change of choice, but one of necessity, I decided to look at the positive side. For one thing, Dad and George, after years of being apart, were back together; and for another, it would now be easier to justify taking California vacations. The most important of all the positives to come out of their move was that Dad's health showed steady improvement after he left.

Winter that year had been cold and bitter, but at times it also had its warmer moments. In a way, Dad's move helped me to continue to grow and to change. As I became more in charge of my life, I began to view each day with new hope and excitement.

Part Five

≈

SPRINGTIME

When Living Things Blossom

CHAPTER 14

~

AND THE SEASONS PASSED

Growing Older and Hopefully Wiser

Winter was enjoyable, with its holidays, its snow, and all the fun that went with it. But, by the time the season was ready to come to an end following Mother Nature's plan, I too was ready. There is a beauty in the changing of the seasons that I enjoy when I allow myself that pleasure.

During the period when I was sad and lonely, each day felt like a year. After learning to like myself, the pleasures of life came easier to me, and time seemed to move more quickly.

My later teen years were interesting for me. For one thing, I went on to college. I wasn't in the top of my class as far as smarts were concerned, but I wasn't at the bottom either. College was a real trip for me. Many of the kids I met were either into their crazy phase like Marty had been, or were loners, and frightened as I used to be. In a way it was easier for me to understand because I had lived through what they were then experiencing. I was a lot more selective when it came to friends than many of the kids. Some wanted so desperately to belong, but my focus was somewhat different.

It was in some ways a rough four years because I had to work hard at maintaining the grades that I wanted. Some kids could breeze through their classes with A's, but I had to study till all hours to do well. College taught me a lot about motivation and how rewarding it could be. I knew what I wanted, and also knew that no one was going to hand it to me. My sense of personal accomplishment when I graduated was a real high for me. Long after forgetting some of my other learning, the value of goal setting and motivation stayed with me.

Five years after having graduated from college I was married. My daydreaming with Clarence had finally paid off. The wedding was great. Everyone was there, including George and Linda, Dad and Marian, Mom and Fred, and of course all of our friends. Mom gave us our old house as a wedding present; nothing could have been more appreciated. The house where I was raised now belonged to me and my new family. Mom and Fred decided that they preferred condo living, since that house had too many memories of her life with Dad.

The generational torch, so to speak, with all of its learning, continues to be passed on. Married life was fantastic. Being able to share my life with the person I loved was everything I dreamt it might be, and more. It got even better when our first son was born. He was both the ugliest and the most beautiful baby I had ever seen. The feelings I experienced as a father were beyond description. I took pride in every change that took place in his young life. Sometimes when I was alone with him, I prayed that as he grew up he would feel less pain than I had. As a part of my prayers I promised that I would often let him know that I loved him. It was important to me that he'd never need to wonder about how I felt. In my heart I also knew that I would do everything I could to understand him and his needs. I didn't want him ever to have to say, "Why can't anyone hear me?"

A few years later our second son was born, and then our daughter. My wife and I agreed that our well-rounded family was complete.

My eldest son is now entering his pre-teen years, and I'm proud to say that he, his brother, and sister are happy children. My family means more to me than anything I could have imagined. And yet enjoying my quiet time, alone with my thoughts, is also important to me.

Today, the house is still, and more importantly my mind is also quiet. The tall tree in the back yard once again is showing off its new buds, announcing the arrival of spring. Being older, happier, and wiser, I can now look back at my life's experiences with laughter, even though some of them didn't seem too humorous at the time. Feeling my emotional strings being pulled by sensitive situations from my past still moves me today, as they did then.

The seasons don't seem to care; they just continue to change, unaffected by the passing years and the events of my life. Some things never seem to change. For one thing, I'm still watching the big oak which has stood tall and strong all these years in the back yard. I'm not sure why this tree has been so important to me, but I know that it has. I feel a special bond with it. In a way, it's almost like a good friend, one whom I've grown up with and who has always been there with me. I admire its quiet strength and its state of constant change. Its blossoms are green now, reminding me of how lovely springtime is. This time of year has always been special to me. It's a time when living things take root and begin to change and to grow. I've sure had my share of change, but then that's what life is all about.

Speaking of change, a few springtimes back, my wife and I decided to spend Easter vacation with the California branch of our family. Our trip was quite an experience for us all. We left home with a chill still in the air, and arrived in Los Angeles in eighty degree weather. I thought that this would be a reunion to top all reunions, and it was. George and Linda and their two children, Dad and Marian, my wife and I and our three children, were all together. I was happy to see Dad looking so well. He was so excited about seeing us that he carried on with an abundance of energy. I had to remind him kiddingly that the fountain of youth was to be found in Florida, not California, according to Ponce de Leon.

Upon our arrival, Dad insisted that we quickly change into our bathing suits and check out the beach at Santa Monica. We convinced him that tomorrow was another day, and besides, our jet lag had caught up with us. I realized how excited he was to be living in California and how much he wanted to share it with us. I felt excited too, only I was feeling the joy of us being together again. We spent that spring vacation enjoying each other's company and seeing some of the sights as well.

Dad insisted on taking his grandchildren to Disneyland. George and I managed very nicely to duck that trip, so that we could have some time alone. Both of us wanted the opportunity for just the two of us to visit, so we helped pack everyone into the station wagon for their trip. How they all squeezed in it's hard to say, but they did, and off they went happy as could be. Dad, the proud grandfather, could be heard singing to the children, "We're off to see the Wizard, the wonderful Wizard of Oz..."

I'm sure that nobody was going to stop him long enough to tell him that the Wizard of Oz had nothing to do with Disney. We knew that everyone would have a great time, including Dad.

George and I drove to a pretty spot near the ocean, that he told me was one of his favorite places. We climbed up some large boulders to a rocky ledge that allowed us a spectacular view of the waves pounding against the shoreline below us. It was a sight that he was sure I wouldn't get to see often, since there wasn't an ocean to be found within a thousand miles of my home. In a way, it reminded me a little of my spot above the lake. I asked him if he had specially arranged this scene for my visit.

"Hey, brother," he responded, "this is Hollywood. We can create wonders like this without any difficulty. And it wouldn't take any longer to provide you with a desert scene, as well."

"Well then, with all this great stuff you Hollywoodians can produce, how about coming up with a chocolate ice cream soda, served right here on the rocks."

"Jamie, I said we can produce wonders, not miracles. However, my brother, if you can wait till we climb down I'll produce the greatest ice cream soda you've ever had. It'll be a true miracle, at least as far as taste is concerned."

George and I took pleasure in the renewal of our closeness as brothers. Reentry for us into our relationship was at first full of puns and joshing, which was our safe way of reconnecting.

Soon our joking turned more serious and the warmth we felt for each other showed itself once again. After we got started there was no stopping us. Making up for lost time, we talked for hours and yet it seemed like minutes. We agreed that in spite of the distance we would make an effort to stay in touch more often.

We went on and on, covering every subject, including Dad and his family, and Mom and hers, and then we brought each other up to date on what was happening in our lives. I was excited to hear that George had been promoted to a full professorship at the University. This had been one of his long term goals after he decided that he didn't want to do clinical work in psychology. At first, the family was surprised when he changed his major once again, after planning for such a long time to become a Psychotherapist. Somewhere along the line he realized that what he wanted for himself was research and teaching, so that became his thing.

George had a favorite expression, which from time to time he repeated to me, even though it didn't make much sense until I got older. When he explained his decision making process for revising his career goals, he expressed it again, "First, I did as much analysis as I could, weighing all of the pro's and con's, then when it got right down to it and I still felt somewhat confused, I did what usually works best for me, I—"

At that point I interrupted him, "I know George, you trusted your feelings."

"Well, I'm glad to see that some of me has rubbed off on you, Jamie. You're darn right I trusted my feelings, and you know what, my feelings haven't let me down too often."

Although I enjoyed kidding George about how he was

beginning to sound like Dad, with all of his words of wisdom, I couldn't deny that his "trust your feelings" belief had worked for me, too. In following his own advice, which obviously had worked for him, Professor English was very comfortable indeed with his work, his decision, and his life.

How we ever climbed up on those rocks, I'm not too sure. All I know is that I had one heck of a time climbing down. My helpful brother the prof wasn't very comforting as he kept reminding me that I must be getting old. There was some truth in his kidding, for we were both getting older. The gray in his hair was almost unreal to me, for my memory of him was still as the kid I admired and who also happened to be my older brother.

We spent a lot of time together during the last part of our vacation, visiting and sharing almost nonstop. I wanted to store up as much as I could of the love I felt from my family in California, for it would have to hold me until we could be together once again.

CHAPTER 15

~

SOME THINGS DON'T SEEM TO CHANGE

Learning from Happiness and Pain

My California visit was over, adding yet another memory to be cherished. Our flight home was a reflective one for me. I remained quiet and within my thoughts as I tried to sort out what had been said and what had gone unsaid. I felt good about us returning to our home and our lives that mean so much to us. But I also felt sad, knowing that I would miss that part of the family who were thousands of miles away.

Clarence met us at the airport and drove us home. I was thankful for his company that first evening and we sat and talked until late. I told him of our wonderful visit and my sad feelings at needing to leave. My ability to share with Clarence helped to reconfirm what I already knew: that even though Dad and George and their families were important to me, my place was here with my family and friends.

Although some people might think that I live too much in

the past, I feel that my past has inspired me. I learned some important lessons from both the painful and the happy events in my life. Perhaps in part I do live in the past, and yet it's those thoughts and beautiful memories which help enrich my experiences of today. I enjoy each day of my life, living them all with no unresolved mysteries from my past. Even the bad and lonely times of my youth served their purpose well, for the learning they provided has added much to nourish my growth.

Today, my thoughts return to my friends. The years have been good to us. Many changes have taken place, but that's not unusual in the passing of thirty years. Thinking of changes once again reminded me of Marty. He and his wild incident that stood the school on end that day, so many years ago. Who could ever forget him or what he did? Those of us who were there will never forget it, especially Marty. It was a major turning point in his life. He made a lot of changes for himself as he got older and left his old patterns behind. I think the most important lesson he learned was that trying so hard to be accepted didn't work for him. Directing his energy towards improving himself was the real payoff; the rest came naturally.

Marty became one of the most popular and well thought of people in our community. Still doing things in a big way, Marty graduated from high school with honors. He also represented the graduating class at the commencement exercises by presenting the valedictorian address, which he did with style. That was quite a day for Marty and his family. It was also a big event for his friends. Clarence, Diane, and I gloated with pride, for the three of us had been at his side through it all.

Marty found what worked for him, and then stayed with it. For a while it was difficult keeping track of him when he moved out of town to go to college. He was accepted at a major ivy league university, and then went on to law school. Clarence and I, kiddingly, would brag about how we knew all along that Marty would become a lawyer. After all, with his ability to talk and his showmanship talent, how could he be anything else?

Success stories are often surprising when they happen to people we know. For those of us who grew up with Marty, it would have been difficult to predict. But Marty the bully, who at times was known for his surprises, performed the biggest suprise of all by doing great things with his life. We heard recently of his latest achievement: he had been accepted as a partner in a major New York law firm. I see him from time to time at high school reunions, which he always manages to attend, and we also write to each other to maintain our connection.

Recently I read an article about Marty which I cut out and saved. Our paper spoke of him in flowery terms: "Local home town boy makes good." Our community is proud of Marty and rightfully so. He worked hard to accomplish his goals and deserves the credit he's now getting. Funny thing is that today Marty gets more acceptance than he ever dreamt possible. When I speak to youngsters who complain of how tough and hopeless life is, as we did when we were kids, I don't hesitate to use Marty as a positive example of how one can change. At the same time, deep in my heart, I understand what they're going through and hope that they come out of it as well as we did.

Clarence will always be my best friend. After all, he was

the first person I became close with in my youth. In spite of the short time when we seemed to be growing apart, we are and always will be, inseparable. It's difficult to believe that we've been friends for thirty years. As we grew older our maturity and our years together helped us to become even better friends. There is much to be said for having developed the kind of roots that we did in this town and our connection with one another. I sometimes wonder how long it would have taken me to establish a friendship like ours if I had moved somewhere else.

Looking at what Clarence has done with his life is exciting to me, for he, too, has become successful; in a different way than Marty perhaps, but nonetheless successful. Clarence is very happy doing exactly what he wants. Can anyone hope for more than that? When Clarence graduated from high school he took a somewhat different direction for himself. He wanted more than anything else to own his own business and to be his own boss. So, instead of going to college, he went to work. He learned all he could about business and saved his money until the day came when he was able to open his own place.

Clarence now owns the first and only combination book store and coffee house in our city. In a way, he has brought a little bit of Greenwich Village to our quiet town, and we love it. It's the kind of place that people enjoy going to for good books, friendship, and the unusual foods and coffees he offers. Besides enjoying his work, Clarence has become financially comfortable.

The dreams we had as kids of remaining close not only did come true, but our wives are good friends as well. Clarence married Jenny, a beautiful young woman who came to our town from New York. At the time, she was seeking a temporary retreat from her busy life as an editor in the book publishing field. Jenny enjoys telling how she left the hustle and bustle of the big city to find herself, and in doing so, found Clarence as well. "Not too shabby; I got two for the price of one," she's quick to add.

She went to work for Clarence, his business being the only one in town that she could relate to. Her love of books and the free spirited artistic environment of Clarence's shop moved her to seek employment with him. In her playful way Jenny told Clarence that had he been a better businessman, like some of her city slicker friends, he would have realized that she would have gone to work for him without pay after having experienced the magic of his place. Clarence's response is always the same, "I'm a lot better businessman than you may think, Ms. City Slicker. I would have doubled your salary if you would have asked for it, once I experienced the magic of you."

The way Clarence and Jenny met and fell in love could compete with any of the love stories in the books that can be found in their store. It was, as they say, a happening: two genuine people with similar interests found each other, and the rest is history. They were married that same year, and needless to say, Jenny never left our town; her temporary retreat became a permanent one.

I don't believe I ever saw Clarence happier or more content than he is now. He found meaning in his life, which in darker days he thought might never be there for him. Jenny also found her niche in life. With Clarence's encouragement she is now doing what she's always wanted to do, writing books, instead of editing for others.

At times, when I'm in a philosophical mood, I wonder about such things as success and how it's measured. I think of having heard it defined in terms of accumulated wealth, position, or status. When I see the happiness that Clarence and Jenny have, there's no doubt in my mind that they have achieved what they desired. That, to me, is what success is all about.

There are two remaining characters from my past who haven't been fully brought up to date. One was that kid with freckles who now is an adult with freckles. As an adult, I've gotten used to both my freckles and my name. Jamie sort of grew on me, but I insist that the children in my class call me Mr. English. I'm now a school teacher, at, of all places, my old alma mater Farnsworth Junior High.

Everything in life changes, and yet some things tend to repeat themselves. I began at Farnsworth and here I am back again. Of course my situation is rather different. Now they don't call me "scrub." Hearing that term with each new group of seventh graders, I can empathize with them, but I know that they will survive it just as I did. And who knows, maybe for some lucky young fellow a Diane will come to his aid and help change his life. Dr. Goodson is no longer principal. He retired before I started teaching there. I regret not having been able to work with him, however, I was lucky in respect to someone else from my past. Miss Richards is still teaching at Farnsworth, but she is now Mrs. Brandon, having married a number of years ago. But when she and I are alone, I tell her that she'll always be Miss Richards to me. We work well together. Oh, yes, and something else that hasn't changed: I'm still learning from her.

My attention was abruptly distracted by a voice from

downstairs... "Jamie, your breakfast is ready and you'll be late for school if you don't get your act on the road."

Speaking of how things don't change, for that split second it sounded like Mom calling out to me. It wasn't her though. It's my wife Diane. Persistence and love paid off for us; Diane and I continued our relationship in spite of that period in high school when her parents thought she should date other guys. We hung in there and waited, but we never stopped loving each other. Our love and respect for one another continues to grow. The only squabble we've had that has lasted more than a day involved our son Tony. When he was born Diane wanted to name him Jamie Jr., but I put my foot down. She conceded, and I can happily say I've never heard him complain about being called Tony.

I kissed Diane and the children goodbye as I rushed out the front door on my way to school. As usual, I was running behind schedule, but that's sort of the norm for me. After all, my neighbors are used to seeing me jog to work, so why should I disappoint them? Jogging hasn't affected my ability to observe and enjoy the scenery on the way. I'm still able to appreciate the homes and the lovely trees with their spring colors on the parkways as I go by.

In running past Marty's old block, where he used to live and play, in my mind's eye I can almost see him just as he was. His sneakers are still untied, and his cap is tilted so much to one side that it looks like it might fall off at any moment. He's tossing his ball up into the air and I can hear him shouting to me as he had done so many times in the past, "Hey, Jamie baby, wanna play?"

I couldn't help myself, my face breaking into a childish grin, as I answered in a forceful voice that only I could hear, "I sure do, Marty, I sure do."

Part Six

∾

THROUGH ALL THE SEASONS OF OUR LIVES

CHAPTER 16

⌐

EXPLORING HAPPINESS
AND GROWTH

The tree in Jamie's back yard took root, grew tall, and became strong over the years, unaffected by the changing seasons. In spite of some negative conditions during its early years, it managed to do well, Other trees born of the same seeds were not able to withstand the difficult times and wilted away. Jamie's tree, like Jamie, grew even stronger from those experiences.

As a part of their growth, both trees and people require nourishment from sources outside themselves to stimulate their development. If they have been well nurtured, the likelihood is they will mature independently strong. Loving care is important during those growing years and beyond. With this kind of support, one can enjoy basking in the sun (the pleasurable side of life) and when the need arises, be able to handle the stormiest of days (the unpleasant times), as well.

In today's society, something is missing in preparing youth for their future growth and independence. Painstakingly they are schooled and guided toward career goals, which are quite important, as we all need to acquire skills for making a living. However, little is offered along with career training to develop personal relating skills.

Resolving conflicts, developing relationships, parenting, or even coping with stress, are all absent from early educational curriculum. Expectations seem to be that these functions come naturally, with the essential learning acquired through experience. Unfortunately, the trial and error approach has been extremely costly, resulting in long term problems affecting individuals and families. The development of these personal skills is necessary for us to be able to live independently, or share our lives with others. If relating is important, as I believe it is, then these skills should be included in the continuing educational process, along with career planning and academic skills.

In looking at your own situation, it would be a cop out to use your lack of "social education" as an excuse for not improving yourself. Personal responsibility is the primary issue, for it is never too late to learn or to improve oneself. Doing the best we can often means doing it in spite of our environment, and realizing that for every negative there is a positive. Personal accomplishments are usually more rewarding when we have been challenged by and are able to overcome obstacles in our path.

Clarence became successful as he grew older by finding true peace within himself, and with it, happiness in life. There was no magic involved in his success. He had no great need for wealth or power; his wants and needs were simple. His greatest desires were to love and to be loved, and to do the kind of work that was most satisfying to him.

Happiness is something everyone wants and searches for. However, people often overlook the one place where happiness can be found: within oneself. The fable of Prince Charming describes how the prince rides up on his white horse and whisks some lonely girl off to eternal happiness. Each of us has the power to control our own feelings. When we can accept that happiness and contentment come from within, it will also be easier to understand the need for working on the self instead of waiting for somebody or something to make one's life complete.

With a better understanding of the self, interaction with others will come easier, and the elusive butterfly of happiness that everyone keeps chasing may come to rest on your shoulder.

CHAPTER 17

〜

IMPROVING YOUR RELATIONSHIPS THROUGH POSITIVE ACTION

Making Choices for Yourself

Jamie's story had a happy ending, which isn't unusual in fiction. In the real world, where life's situations are experienced, not created, problems aren't always resolved that easily, without making the choice to do so.

Some people wrap themselves in negativity and are constantly unhappy. They choose to accept their fate, based on how life looks and feels during difficult times. Seeing no glimmer of light or hope at the end of their tunnel of life, they minimize responsibility for their pain and for doing anything about it. Although these people make a choice to live out their self-fulfilling prophecy, they can often be heard asking, "Why is this happening to me?"

The truth is that no one needs to be a passive participant in the adventure of living. By accepting responsibility for the choices you make, you become more actively involved in how your life unfolds. Even people who seem unable to make a decision for themselves, and have others do it for them, have made a choice: to have someone else make the choice for them and to remove themselves from the process.

Seeking guidance when making critical decisions is wise, especially when others have more experience or knowledge on a particular issue. However, it's one thing to be open to input or advice, and another to only rely on others to make all your decisions.

For parents, fostering your children's independence and guiding them toward making informed decisions and intelligent choices on their own is a constructive path to follow. Allowing children to make decisions is an important factor in their maturing process.

It is easier to share opinions and feelings which encourage making positive choices in an atmosphere of mutual trust and respect. When this is missing within the relationship, expressing views and being heard are restricted. Jamie was often reminded that children must show respect for their parents by not speaking until spoken to. It is difficult to respect or listen to the advice of anyone who regulates you into silence when you have a need to be heard.

If you find yourself limiting another person's ability to interact with you, make a conscious choice to alter your behavior by listening more and advising less. Parents, wanting so much for their children to learn from their experiences, sometimes try to impose their learning and choices upon them. Although these adults may have the best intentions, this approach is not usually effective. The best learning you can provide for your teenagers would be to become a good role model. Offer direction with understanding and yet be firm and consistent in enforcing the important guidelines of your home. With a good supportive environment, teens will be open to learning from you, as well as from their own experiences.

One of the most valuable gifts parents can give their children is to help them become independent decision makers. By learning to make intelligent choices for themselves without being dependent, they will acquire a strength they can utilize throughout their lives.

For you teenagers who find you have made a choice to reject all input from your parents and teachers, it would be worthwhile to ask yourself, "Am I so much smarter than all the adults in my life and therefore don't need to listen, or am I overreacting, and if so, why?" Chances are, your answer may be connected to wanting to "prove" how grown-up and independent you are, which may include showing all adults that you don't need to listen to them.

The course your life takes is directly connected to the choices you make. Whether one does something positive which will be of value, or something negative that will prove harmful, is a matter of individual choice. Knowing the difference between the two and making the best choices may be the truest sign of one's maturity.

Examining the Poor Me Attitude

For adolescents and parents who find your relationship stretched to the limit, now may be the time for you to review and make possible changes. It's never too late to examine how you relate to others, or they to you. A good place to begin is by looking at the choices you've been making, and at your responsibility for what takes place within the relationship. During this process it is helpful to maintain a clear and open mind. Blaming others or yourself does nothing to resolve your differences and often causes anger.

If your situation is painful and feels like your world is falling apart around you, hang onto your hope that the situation will get better. Then take some action to make it happen. The choice between, "it's time to move on" or "stay where you are" is yours to make. You may know people who seem to thrive on sympathy. They choose to remain in their "poor me" place as self-identified "victims," complaining how terrible life has been to them. Yet, sadness and pain are not limited to them alone, for at one time or another everyone experiences these feelings.

Some people choose to move from their painful place after living with it for an appropriate time; others choose to remain there. For those who remain, there's probably a payoff which motivates them to stay. Their reward may be in the attention they receive or having some less obvious need satisfied.

Making the most of your life is your responsibility. It would be foolish to expect that you will always be free of problems, and that you will be continuously happy. It would be equally foolish to expect the opposite extreme. Perhaps the answer lies somewhere in between.

There are incidents which occur that may be beyond your control, such as: incurable illness, disabilities, or death of a loved one. However, even in those situations there are choices to be made as to how you will react to those crises. Individuals identified medically as permanently disabled, depending on how they view themselves, may not be disabled at all. In many cases, their feats of emotional and physical endurance overshadow their so-called physical disabilities.

An example of this is Jeff Keith, a young man who lost a leg to cancer at age 12. In spite of his "handicap," he completed a 3,300 mile run across the United States. His purpose was to raise funds for the Cancer Society ($120,000 in contributions were received). Also, he wanted to encourage those confined in hospitals and rehab centers to recognize that their disabilities need not limit them from living their lives to the fullest. Jeff Keith was quoted as saying, "Cancer can be beat. I'm not physically handicapped, I'm physically challenged." We can learn much from the positive choices he made for himself.

Everyone carries their own form of disability, in one way or another. Prior conditioning can play a major role in developing these handicaps. Yet, handicaps are often used as an excuse for staying in a negative place. Recognize for yourself that conditioning can be overcome if you have the desire to do so. How you react to situations, with a poor me response, or the desire to move to a better place, is connected to your attitude.

166

Making positive choices is an important part of the process of moving forward in your life. Marty's choice of doing wild things to get attention and acceptance resulted in negative feedback and ridicule. Clarence's method of getting his parents to listen almost resulted in his death, and Jamie's choice made him very lonely. The direction you take in life, or the changing of that course later, is within your personal power.

Three key factors to remember are: don't give up when the going gets rough (hang in there); assume responsibility for helping to resolve your problems (let go of the poor me role); and use your choices wisely to move yourself to a place of strength.

Creating Your Reality Through Positive Beliefs

All aspects of your life are affected by your beliefs. The subconscious mind, like a computer, absorbs data offered to it and accepts it as fact. When either positive or negative beliefs are dominant, the subconscious mind directs that information into personal action, reflecting the influence of that belief. Your actions or behavior, connected to your belief system, remains with you until they are replaced by stronger beliefs. That is why individuals with low self-esteem, who do nothing to change their view of themselves, stay with their negative feelings and actions for a long time.

If you feel unhappy with yourself and how you relate to others, the best thing you might do (in addition to seeing a counselor if you're having difficulty on your own) would be to start working on replacing old negative beliefs with new more positive ones.

A good place to begin is to convince yourself that your current beliefs and actions can be modified if your desire to do so is strong enough. Changing what was previously accepted by the subconscious involves inputting new data and repeating that information on a regular basis. The repetition is necessary to move your new thoughts into new beliefs.

One method for developing and inputting new beliefs is called "affirmations" (making positive declarations to oneself). The procedure for using affirmations is to prepare a positive statement concerning something you would like to see happen that involves you. That statement, written in the present tense (as opposed to a future desire) becomes your affirmation. By repeating it with feeling, in a direct and positive way, you affirm that statement to your subconscious mind, which in time accepts it as fact.

Place your written affirmation where it can be seen, like on your mirror, and read it often. Repeat it at least twice a day, when you wake up and before going to sleep. Affirmations can be used to help attain things you want for yourself, and which are affected by your own abilities and beliefs.

Use the following affirmation for improving your self-esteem, or create one using your own words.

> *Each day I become more in touch with who*
> *I am and what I want.*
> *I am unique.*
> *I am special.*
> *I deserve and will receive all that I truly*
> *want for myself.*

Visual imagery (images created in your mind) can also be used with affirmations to improve your self-image. The Chinese expression, "A picture is worth a thousand words" applies in helping to reframe negative feelings about oneself into positive beliefs.

Imagery is also beneficial for relieving stress and tension. Try the following exercise when you feel yourself becoming tense. Close your eyes, and imagine yourself in a relaxing place which you have experienced before. To add to your relaxation, take three slow, deep breaths, which will have a calming effect on your body. The value of relaxation and deep breathing can be seen in its application with expectant mothers. They learn to relax during childbirth as an effective means of lessening their tension and pain during labor and delivery.

As you continue to use this imagery, seeing yourself totally relaxed and with the help of your deep breathing, you will create the reality of your imagery.

Utilizing visual imagery to improve your self-image (how you see yourself) involves the same process. Do your deep breathing exercise to relax yourself. Then, with your eyes closed, call on the words of your affirmation to help you develop images of yourself in your mind. See yourself as a person who is indeed special and who truly deserves the best of everything. As you continue to view yourself as worthwhile, and believe it, your subconscious mind will accept this new data while leaving go of the old programming. You will soon begin to feel the results of these new beliefs as they affect all parts of your life.

The mind has infinite power, but we only use a small fraction of its capacity. By understanding that your belief system directly affects everything you do and say, you will be better able to utilize the power or your mind to bring positive changes into your life.

Relieving Stress and Tension

Everyone at one time or another experiences stress as a normal part of everyday living. As people interact with one another, live in a busy environment, or undergo changes, stress will be there. Since it cannot be eliminated, the best strategy for surviving its negative effects is to learn to cope with it. Coping is the ability to handle negative situations and people with a minimum amount of lingering harmful effects.

In learning to cope with stress, become aware of how you are affected by people or situations that are displeasing to you. Then evaluate your options for changing how they affect you. Of the three options to select from, one is most effective. The first option, "avoid it," sometimes works. Yet as a general rule, avoiding it is not best, since you cannot always run from people and situations that are stressful to you. The second option, "change it," usually is not workable, since you cannot change other people, and many situations may be beyond your control. The third and best option is to "change your reaction" to those things and people that disturb you. To change your reaction to the negatives in your life you will need to overcome some of your current learned behavior.

Giving away your power to control your own feelings,

will leave you in a weakened position. Yet, this is exactly what happens when another person's negative behavior causes a strong reaction in you. Learning to take charge of your reactive behavior will leave you feeling happier and healthier.

Venting your feelings to release the pressure of what's bothering you is a healthy way to relieve the build-up of stress and tension. When releasing negative feelings, you must be considerate of your impact upon others. Yelling at and blaming people for how they supposedly made you feel is not a good way to deal with your anger. Letting the other person know that you're upset and describing how you feel is a much better course of action. You need to take responsibility for how you feel without placing blame on someone else. No one other than yourself can make you feel angry, sad, or happy, without you allowing it.

Storing up feelings without release can have explosive results. As an example, picture a tea kettle boiling on the stove, with all of its openings sealed. Without releasing the pressure that builds up within it, eventually it will explode. Without a release for your pressure, you too, will experience some form of explosive reaction. It may come in the form of a verbal or physical attack on someone who happened to be there at the time, or it could result in some physical and/or emotional illness. Releasing your feelings a little at a time, as you experience them, is an effective way to minimize the build-up of pressure. Using this approach will help you prevent emotional blowups, and will also relieve the stress and tension you feel.

Learning to Accept Yourself and Others

Having dreams for your future is healthy, but creating unrealistic expectations for yourself or others sets the stage for disappointment and unhappiness. The Serenity Prayer expresses this concept very well:

God grant me the serenity to accept
the things I cannot change,
courage to change the things I can,
and wisdom to know the difference.

The concept of expectations and acceptance is important to understand. It's best to help others by offering them guidance and love without having expectations for changing them. The truth is, we can't change anyone else; we can only change ourselves. Learning to accept people for who they are, without expectations (how you feel they should be) can be difficult, especially with those you care about. Yet, accepting a person for who and what they are doesn't mean you agree with their attitudes or actions. It does mean you can allow for some form of relationship with that person. Remember, unrealistic expectations will set you up for frustration and anger.

There are some ways you can indirectly effect change in other people. Although you can't change others, you do have the ability to influence them, thus indirectly effecting their change.

Positive role models provide the best form of influence. Through your life you will find special people who influence and motive you to make changes. You may now be experiencing some people in your life who you consider strict or unreasonable at times. In the years to come you may acknowledge and appreciate these people for holding firm and being consistent at a time when you needed it most.

There is a significant difference between influencing someone else's desire to change through positive role modeling and guidance, and demanding their change because of your expectations of how they should be. One works well; the other produces a negative response.

Evaluating Rules and Limits

We all have a need for rules or laws we can live buy. It takes more effort on the part of parents to establish rules and limits and to enforce them, than it does to assume an attitude of indifference, such as, "Let them do what they want." Young people prefer having limits set for them. When parents are passive regarding setting limits, this may be viewed as a lack of caring.

Parents who provide what is referred to as "tough love" at a time when it is needed are truly loving parents. They make the difficult choice of taking strict corrective action against their children to prevent the continuation of unlawful and destructive behavior. They do this knowing it is best for their children, while setting aside their own sympathetic feelings.

Other parents may respond to their children's self-destructive ways by satisfying their own needs for reducing their feelings of guilt. Their lack of action can be harmful to the long-term welfare of their children. This overly sympathetic position and bail out from punishment often distorts their children's values regarding rewards and punishment. When this bail out behavior is repeated in one form or another, it reinforces the teens' undesirable behavior. The negative actions of the teens receive rewards (attention) without retribution, which motivates their ongoing pattern.

There is a dual responsibility for parents and teens regarding rules and limits. Young adults, as long as they live with and depend on their parents, need to abide by the rules of their home. Parents have a responsibility, as well, to establish sensible rules for their children to live by. Healthy relationships are built on fairness, with consideration for one another, and with limits that are carefully established and well defined.

These healthy relationships are usually dynamic in their structure. A dynamic relationship is one that is flexible instead of rigid. It allows for movement and growth, without manipulation. Within such a relationship the participants are willing to explore themselves individually and together. This is a positive approach, as opposed to being judgmental or critical of the other person.

When you can look at your own role within the relationship without blaming the other person, you will become more objective and fair regarding family disputes. Rules which govern the household can then be periodically evaluated and modified as needed. The adolescent's need for emotional and intellectual growth, as well as for greater independence, can then be respected. Parents who encourage independence will allow the cords which have bound their teens to them to be lengthened. This action will help all concerned to take pride in their family unit as it matures. The end result may be the enjoyment of a special closeness with their young adults whose growth they have encouraged.

Developing a Support System

Clarence, Marty, and Jamie all wanted to be heard, understood, and accepted. Yet, during their earlier years, what they wanted most they were unable to get. At times everyone needs someone they can talk to, without judgment or criticism. The key to a loving relationship is the support given to one another when the need arises.

Having a supportive adult who teens can communicate with is important to their well-being. Dr. Balding pointed out that communication must include listening, as well as speaking. When a person is hurting, they don't need advice; they need someone caring to listen to them.

Youth Law News, January-February 1985 reported that on an annual basis at least 7,000 teenagers kill themselves, and 400,000 attempt suicide. The government's General Accounting Office, in 1983, estimated that one million children were not living at home; one-half were forced out, and the other half were runaways. A survey made in 1983, of 16,000 high school seniors nationwide reported that 63% had tried an illicit drug, and 40% were using drugs other than marijuana. This data reflects upon the problems in the family, and the inability of these young people to find someone they can trust who will hear them and offer positive guidance. It also sadly reveals how teenagers make the immature choice of a highly destructive path in dealing with their problems.

On the positive side, trends reflect that parents are becoming more responsive to the feelings of young adults, and greater numbers of adolescents are rejecting drugs and peer pressure. Parent/teen and adolescent support groups sponsored by local PTA's and schools are contributing to improved communication. Where this forum is available for a release of feelings in a non-destructive way, antagonistic and rebellious behavior is greatly reduced. When parents can get rid of their pain verbally, there is less need for acting our their anger.

Let's Talk About Divorce

Many young people are experiencing divorce in their families. In some cases they are also going through the re-marriage of one or both of their parents. This major change to their family structure produces feelings of sadness, anger, guilt, and even rejection in the children. Jamie had a strong reaction to his parents' separation and to meeting his father's new friend Marian.

How and when divorce is communicated between parents and children can affect the entire family's adjustment to this change. Children's reaction to the news and the difficulty they experience is apt to be more intense and prolonged when the event occurs without their being prepared for it.

In Jamie's situation he was not made aware of what was about to take place until it actually happened. Although the information communicated to Jamie was handled well by his parents, the timing was not.

When parents do not effectively communicate with their teenage children about issues which affect everyone in the family, they usually are assuming the news will be too painful for their children. This protective attitude reflects a lack of trust in their children's ability to handle unhappy feelings and to overcome them.

If young people are to grow and become emotionally strong, they must learn to accept sensitive and sometimes painful situations as well as pleasant ones. After all, life does not consist of only happy events. There is a similarity in the process of helping young adults develop emotional strength and what takes place with babies as they go through their normal childhood illnesses. The baby, through its experiences, develops a stronger immunity to diseases; the young adult, through their experiences, becomes better able to deal with the reality and the adversities of life.

Very often the child's reaction to their parents' divorce is "they had no right to do this to me." Parents go through a tremendous amount of pain in making their decision to no longer live together. I have never known of a case where parents get a divorce because they want to punish their children. Young people must learn to trust their parents and the actions they take regarding divorce. This is not an easy decision for

177

anyone, but when it becomes more difficult for parents to live together then apart, the action they take is often better for all concerned.

An important part of the healing process for you young people is to express your feelings. There is no better release for what is bothering you than to talk about it. Letting your parents know how you feel will also help them to better understand what you are going through.

There is no question that divorce is painful. However, young people everywhere are surviving the experience. They are learning not to blame themselves as the cause of their parents' actions. They are also becoming aware that divorce does not need to mean they have lost a parent or a parent's love. The "Blended Family," created when two families and their children come together through marriage, can and often does enlarge the circle of love and caring.

Young and old alike can better deal with the immediate pain accompanying shocking or unhappy news when they trust one another, communicate in an open and truthful way, and share feelings of both happiness and pain.

Part Seven

∾

REMOVING THE BARRIERS TO COMMUNICATION

THROUGH INTERACTION WE BECOME CONNECTED

Establishing a supportive environment that will allow for nonjudgmental relating is essential to the adolescent/parent relationship. When the atmosphere at home does not provide this support, teenagers may turn to some form of self-destructive or apathetic behavior. This behavior will often result in their parents' frustration and anger. As a part of this negative cycle, everyone may distance themselves from one another to avoid the pain they are experiencing. Marty chose an outgoing disruptive path in his need for acceptance by his peers; whereas Jamie and Clarence turned inward, becoming loners as they tried to avoid everyone. In spite of their different reactions, they all had the same basic concerns: feelings of low self-esteem, of not being accepted, and of not having anyone they could turn to who would listen. (Why can't anyone hear me?)

The process of distancing includes shutting down communication and feelings. Closing oneself off from feeling pain also restricts the give and take of positive and loving feelings. When this happens, all involved are left feeling alone, unloved and unwanted.

The following points of discussion offer you a way to start removing those barriers which keep parents and adolescents separated. Through interaction we remain connected; without it there is no relationship. Because of prior conditioning, many people are afraid of conflict, and therefore avoid dealing with any confrontation. If this applies to you, remember Dr. Balding's statement: "Fears don't go away on their own; you must face them head on, one at a time, and then get past them."

Approach the points of discussion and the interaction that will be a part of it, with the desire for improving your relationship. Make this a positive experience and don't use it to blame each other. There is a tendency in relationships with problems to cling to the unhappy memories. If your relationship is to improve, you must be willing to forgive and to move on.

Your discussion will be more productive and meaningful if "YOU" statements are replaced with "I" statements. As an example, what would it feel like if someone said to you, "YOU make me clam up so that I can't tell you what's going on inside of me"? Blaming statements are self-defeating because they cause the other person to feel attacked and to react defensively. This type of communication prevents a positive outcome and doesn't allow anyone to be heard. Now experience what the same information feels like by saying, "I sometimes feel uncomfortable telling you what's going on inside of me." In this example, the person speaking is sharing how they feel. This type of communication doesn't bring about an angry reaction, for no one is being blamed. Non-blaming "I" statements also provide clearer communication. Without defensive or angry responses, people are able to better hear one another.

I recommend you begin your discussion while the story is still fresh in your mind. Keep unrealistic expectations to a minimum, remain patient with one another, and open yourself to sharing feelings in a loving way.

DISCUSSION FOR PARENTS AND TEENS

1. This story, about Jamie, his family and friends, is about all kinds of people and what goes on in their lives. What are your feelings about this story? Did you like it, and what part did you like best?

2. Which of the characters in the story can you best relate to, and what similarities are there between you and this person?

3. Which character in the story are you least like, and how are you different from that person?

4. What effect did Jamie, Clarence, and Marty's self-esteem have upon their behavior?

5. Have you known people (young or old) who have problems with their self-esteem? Without identifying them by name, what do they do that shows how poorly they feel about themselves?

6. What parts of the story affected you in a sad or happy way, and how were you able to connect those events to your life or the lives of those you know?

7. Do you know anyone who attempted to take his/her life, like Clarence did? How did you feel when you became aware of it? Have you ever had those kind of thoughts? What did you do to overcome these feelings?

8. Have you heard your parents arguing? If so, how did you feel during those times?

9. How well do you and your parents communicate, and what might be done to improve it?

10. How could the level of caring and support in your relationship be improved?

11. Do you find it easier to show your anger instead of your love? If so, why do you think this is true?

12. How might you begin to express what you want from your parent/child?

13. Have unrealistic expectations (how you feel each of you "should be") distanced you from one another? Can you think of some way to improve the situation?

14. Can you understand why fair rules and limits are required within your relationship, and do you feel the limits established are fair? If not, "discuss" how you would like to see them changed, without becoming angry or demanding.

Reaching an agreement on what are fair limits and how they should be changed, are not always reached during the first discussions. Even if you are unable to come to an agreement this time, get in touch with how good it feels to be able to discuss these issues without becoming angry. You can also take pride in knowing that by handling your discussion in a non-demanding way, you have made future discussions easier.

Allowing feelings to flow when they have been shut down may take a little doing, so be patient with one another, and by all means keep working at it. You will see the value for yourselves when the barriers start to come down and love is allowed to flow freely. Relationships are not made or reestablished in a day. They all begin the same way, by taking that first step of being willing to risk and reach out to someone you care about. The important second step takes place when the other person responds. To alter the cry of "Why can't anyone hear me?" to feelings of "I do hear you and I do understand" is an objective worth pursuing.

There is a belief in the Eastern philosophies that the true meaning of life's experiences is not found in the events themselves. Instead, the value comes from the lessons that are learned from those events. Hopefully, you will learn and grow from your experiences and better understand your life's lessons.

May your story have many joyful new beginnings and happy endings on your path through life. And in between, discover the true meaning of success through inner contentment and happinses, by sharing your life with others in harmony. Above all, may you never again need to say, "Why can't anyone hear me?"

RESOURCES

There are many reliable resources available, for both parents and teens, covering a wide variety of problems. Many of the organizations listed below have local chapters nationwide, and their numbers can be obtained from the white pages of your telephone directory. In addition, check the yellow pages of your directory under Mental Health Associations, Social Service Agencies, or specific categories for other resources.

ALCOHOLISM
National Council on Alcoholism
Local chapters nationwide provide information on alcoholism, community education, and treatment referrals.
(800) 3231-PASS Information service for teens and parents in So. Ca.
Al-anon Family Group Headquarters, Inc.
For families of problem drinkers.
Alateen
For teens whose parents are problem drinkers.
P.O. Box 862
Mid Town Station
New York, NY 10018
(212) 302-7240 New York / (213) 387-3158 Los Angeles
Be-Sober Hotline
(800) 237-6237
Alcohol and Drug Helpline
(800) 252-6465

CHILD ABUSE/NEGLECT
Child Help
(800) 422-4453 (24. hr.)
National Child Abuse Hot Line
P.O. Box 630
Hollywood, CA 90028
Information, referrals and crisis counseling relating to support services in the areas of child abuse and neglect, parenting, runaway youth and other family problems.
Parents Anonymous
(800) 421-0353 Nationwide / (800) 352-0386 California
7120 Franklin Ave.
Los Angeles, CA 90046
Self-help for parents who abuse their children or are potential abusers.

Child Abuse Hot Line
(California) Dial "O" and ask for Zenith 21234
National Council on Child Abuse and Family Violence
(800) 222-2000

INCEST/MOLESTATION
Parents United (National Headquarters)
P.O. Box 952
San Jose, CA 95108
(213) 727-4080 (Los Angeles Chapter)
Also: Son/Daughter United and Children United
Group therapy for families where molestation or incest has
occurred.

INFORMATION & REFERRAL SERVICE
Information and Referral Federation
(800) 242-4612 (L.A. County)
Nationwide organization providing information and referrals
regarding human services.

PARENT GROUP
Toughlove
Local chapters nationwide provide support groups for parents
troubled by teen-age behavior.
"Because I Love You" — The Parents Support Group practicing Tough
Love.

RUNAWAYS/MISSING CHILDREN
National Runaway Switchboard
(800) 621-4000 Nationwide / (800) 392-3352 Illinois
24 hr. information and referral service for runaways, throwaways,
and other homeless youth who are 17 and under. Runaways can
contact their family through a message relay service, without
divulging their location.
Child Find Hotline
(800) 426-5678

SEX INFORMATION
VD National Hotline
(800) 227-8921 / (800) 982-5883
Provides telephone counseling,information and treatment referrals
for sexually transmitted diseases,
Los Angeles Sex Information Helpline
(213) 653-1990 (Los Angeles Free Clinic)
Planned Parenthood Clinic
(800) 223-3303

STEP FAMILIES
    Stepfamily Association of America
        (301) 823-7570
        602 E. Joppa Road
        Baltimore, MD 21204
        Support network and national advocate for stepparents, remarried
        parents, and their children.

SUBSTANCE ABUSE
    Families Anonymous
        (chapters nationwide)
        Los Angeles Chapter:
        (818) 989-7842 (24 hr.)
        P.O. Box 528
        Van Nuys, CA 91408
        Self-help groups for families of chemical (substance) abusers
        and related behavioral problems.
    Cocaine (and Crack) Hotline
        (800) COCAINE / (800) 662-HELP
    NFP Drug Information Line
        (800) 554-KIDS
        National Federation of Parents for Drug Free Youth
    NIDA Prevention Information Line
        (800) 638-2045

SUICIDE
    Suicide Prevention Center (chapters nationwide)
        Los Angeles Chapter:
        (213) 381-5111
        Provides 24 hr. "Crisis Line" phone counseling services.
    Metro-Help
        (800) 621-4000
        24-hr. national crisis hotline for suicidal and runaway youth.

YOUTH SERVICES
    Counseling services are provided on a no fee sliding scale basis
    through the following organizations:
        Family Services (including Jewish Family Service and Catholic Social
        Services)
        Child Guidance Clinics

BIBLIOGRAPHY
and
RECOMMENDED READING

Andolfi, Maurizo et al., *The Family Mask*. New York: Bruner/ Mazel, 1983.

Bayard, Robert T., and Jean Bayard. *How to Deal With Your Acting-Up Teenager*. New York: M. Evans & Co., Inc. 1981.

Bell, Ruth. *Changing Bodies, Changing Lives — A Book for Teens on Sex and Relationships*. New York: Random House, 1981.

Berry, Caroline Franklin and Diana Shaw. *Options—The Female Teen's Guide to Coping With the Problems of Today's World*. New York: Anchor Press/Doubleday, 1983.

Bienenfeld, Florence. *Helping Your Child Succeed After Divorce*. Claremont, Ca.: Hunter House Publishers, Inc., 1987.

Bodie, Caryn Frye. *The Feelings Book - Expressing Your Emotions Creatively*. Evergreen, Co.: Cordillera Press, 1988.

Brondino, Jeanne, and Teen/Parent Book Group. *Raising Each Other*. Claremont, Ca.: Hunter House Publishers, Inc., 1988.

Casewit, Curtis W. *The Stop Smoking Book for Teens*. New York: Julian Meisner/Simon & Schuster, 1980.

Clemes, Harris, and Reynold Bean. *Self-Esteem*. New York: Kensington Publishing Corp., 1981.

Eckler, James D. *Step-by-Stepparenting*. Crozet, Va.: Betterway Publications, 1988.

Elchoness, Monte. *Guide to Adolescent Enrichment*. Sepulveda, Ca.: Monroe Press, 1987.

Fassler, David, Michele Lash, and Sally B. Ives. *Changing Families*. Burlington: Waterfront Books, 1988.

Fleming, Alice. *What to Say When You Don't Know What to Say*. New York: Charles Scribner's Sons, 1982.

Frankel, Victor E. *The Unheard Cry for Meaning*. New York: Simon and Schuster, 1978.

French, Alfred P. *Disturbed Children and Their Families*. New York: Human Sciences Press, 1979.

Gardener, Richard A. *The Boys and Girls Book About Divorce*. New York: Bantam, 1983.

Gawain, Shakti. *Creative Visualization*. Mill Valley, Ca.: Whatever Publishing, 1982.

Getzoff, Ann, and Carolyn McClenahan. *Step Kids*. New York: Walker and Company, 1984

Gilbert, Sara. *Trouble at Home*. New York: Lothrop, Lee & Shepard Books, 1981.

Glenbard East Echo. *Teenagers Themselves*. New York: Adama Books, 1984.

Glenn, H. Stephen and Jane Nelson. *Raising Self-Reliant Children*. Rocklin, Ca.: Prima Publishing, 1987.

Hafen, Brent Q. and Kathryn J. Frandsen. *Youth Suicide*. Evergreen Co.: Cordillera Press, 1986.

Haley, Jay. *Uncommon Therapy*. New York: W.W. Norton & Company, 1973.

Hamerlynck, Eric, L. Handy, and E. Mash, eds. *Behavior Modification and Families*. New York: Brunner/Mazel, Inc., 1976.

Harrity, Anne Swayen, and Ann Brey Christensen. *Kids, Drugs and Alcohol*. Crozet, Va.: Betterway Publications., 1987.

Husain, Syed A., and Trish Vandiver. *Suicide in Children and Adolescents*. New York: Spectrum Publications, Inc., 1984

Kolehmainen, Janet, and Sandra Handwerk. *Teen Suicide*. Minneapolis: Lerner Publicatins, 1986.

Lindsay, Jeanne W. *Teenage Marriage*. Buena Park: Morning Glory Press, 1984/1988.

Liss, Jerome. *Family Talk*. New York: Ballantine Books, Inc., 1972.

Malmquist, Carl P. *Handbook of Adolescence*. New York: Jason Aronson Inc., 1985.

Miller, Mary S. *Child Stress*. New York: Doubleday & Co., 1982.

Rench, Janice E. *Teen Sexuality*. Minneapolis: Lerner Publications, 1988.

Richards, Arlene, and Irene Willis. *How to Get It Together When Your Parents Are Coming Apart*. New York: David McKay Company, Inc., 1976.

Rosenbaum, Alvin. *The Young People's Yellow Pages*. New York: Putnam Publishing Group, 1983.

Rubin, Theodore I. *The Angry Book*. New York: Collier Books, 1978.

Samuels, Mike and Nancy Samuels. *Seeing With the Mind's Eye*. New York: Random House Inc., 1979.

Satir, Virginia. *Peoplemaking*. Palo Alto: Science & Behavior Books, Inc., 1972.

Smith, Manuel J. *Kicking the Fear Habit*. New York: The Dial Press, 1977.

Textor, Martin R. *Helping Families With Special Problems*. New York: Jason Aronson, 1983.

Watts, Alan W. *The Meaning of Happiness*. New York: Harper & Row Publishers, Inc., 1979.

INDEX

Dr. Monte Elchoness

ABOUT THE AUTHOR

Monte Elchoness, Ph.D. is a psychotherapist, author and consultant to schools and industry. As a therapist in private practice in Los Angeles, he specializes in family relationships and stress related concerns. As an author he enjoys the challenge of writing about some of our time's more complex issues and presenting them in an easy to understand manner.

As an adjunct to his counseling, he teaches classes and lectures on adolescent concerns, parenting, motivation, self-esteem, and stress management, and has written numerous articles on human behavior.

Dr. Elchoness has also been a pioneer in developing and directing humanistic approaches to industry by improving employee/management relations through participative management programs.

Working with adolescents and writing about their concerns is especially important to Dr. Elchoness, for he recognizes their need to be understood and accepted, and the difficulty they have in communicating these needs to others. He has extensive experience counseling troubled youth, including runaways and throwaways.

Acknowledged for his professional contribution to schools and industry, Dr. Elchoness is listed in "Who's Who in California" and also in "Who's Who in Human Services."

As an accomplished artist, Dr. Elchoness reflects his creativity in all aspects of his work, including the illustrations for *Why Can't Anyone Hear Me?*

Other Books from Monroe Press

COMPLETE TEEN ISSUES/SELF-ESTEEM PROGRAM

WHY CAN'T ANYONE HEAR ME? - A Guide for
Surviving Adolescence (also the program text)
Uses storytelling and metaphors to provide characters
and experiences young people can relate to and discuss.
Focuses on substituting hope, positive actions and the
expression of feelings, for frustration, anger and blame.

GUIDE TO ADOLESCENT ENRICHMENT
(companion tool to *Why Can't Anyone Hear Me?*)
Teacher/counselor curriculum guide for establishing
teen issues/self-esteem groups. A comprehensive action-
oriented program using reading, writing, and relating
exercises to stimulate young people and motivate them to
produce change.

TEEN ISSUES STUDENT WORKBOOK
Consumable Workbook for Self-Esteem Program
For young people to retain their activity sheets and
journal writing for future reinforcement.

— — —

SIGMUND SAYS - A Lighter Look at Freud Through His Id, Ego,
and Super-Ego
Humorous dialogue and creative drawings, combined with
factual data about Freud's theory of the personality,
provide a fun way to learn about Freud and ourselves.

STRESS REDUCTION TRAINING
Deep Relaxation Audio Tape
A viable alternative to burnout and tension, offering a
positive means of reducing the effects of continuous stress.

WHY DO KIDS NEED FEELINGS? - A Guide to Healthy Emotions
Provides families with practical guidance for learning about
feelings, why they are important, and how to express them
appropriately. Includes a story for children and a special
section for adults to help them improve relationships.

PARENT/TEACHER GUIDE to *Why Do Kids Need Feelings?*
Offers structured guidance for use in home or classroom
setting.

ORDER FORM

Please send me the following:

____ *Why Can't Anyone Hear Me?* - A Guide for $10.95
Surviving Adolescence

____ *Guide to Adolescent Enrichment*   18.95

____ *Teen Issues Student Workbook*   6.95

____ *Sigmund Says* - A Lighter Look at Freud   6.95
Through His Id, Ego, and Super-Ego

____ *Stress Reduction Training* - Audio Tape   9.00

____ *Why Do Kids Need Feelings?* - A Guide   9.95
to Healthy Emotions

____ *Parent/Teacher Guide* to *Why Do Kids*   4.95
Need Feelings

Shipping: (10% of order - $2.00 minimum)   _____

Tax: 7% (CA residents only)   _____

Total amount enclosed: $ _____

Name _____

School/Organization _____

Address_____

City _____ State _____ Zip _____

MONROE PRESS
362 Maryville Avenue, #188
Ventura, California 93003-1912
(805) 642-3064